ESSAYS IN SOCIAL ANTHROPOLOGY

Essays in Social Anthropology

RAGHUVIR SINHA

CONCEPT PUBLISHING COMPANY
NEW DELHI-110059

ISBN 81-7022-266-4

First Published 1990

Raghuvir Sinha (*b.* 1933)

Published by
Ashok K umarMittal
Concept Publishing Company
A/15-16, Commercial Block, Mohan Garden
NEW DELHI-110059 (INDIA)

Lasertypeset by
Microtech Advance Printing Systems (P) Ltd.
H-13 Bali Nagar,
NEW DELHI-110015

Printed in India by
A.P. Offset
Naveen Shahdara
DELHI-110032

To

GAYATRI

Contents

Introduction

THIS WORK IS a collection of my Essays in Social Anthropology which were found primarily important for an Indian student trying to know about the development of different concepts, theories and formulations in the field of social anthropology. Today there is a great deal of emphasis on studying modern theories of the Western World which have come in vogue during last few decades. While new innovations and research do provide the basis for any advancement in knowledge, it cannot be denied that the original concepts and theories which gave rise to the discipline of social anthropology have not to be forgotten in the least. It is from this point of view that I had thought it necessary to present afresh the basic knowledge about social anthropology in the form of different essays on various aspects. Each essay is complete in itself, while in an integrated manner it is also interwoven in a coherent manner as a continued dialogue about man and his society.

I hope fervently that these essays will elicit the interest of the students and scholars of social anthropology both, and that both will derive an incentive from this for more research in theoretical social anthropology.

24 September, 1988. RAGHUVIR SINHA

1

Evolutionism in Social Anthropology

Unilinear and Multilinear Evolution

DURING The Last century and to the beginning of the present, a doctrine which had become much popular and much discussed matter of fact , was that of Evolutionism. Evolutionism in the biological as well as the sociological spheres has formed a profound influence, and though the doctrine of evolution in the social field has lost lately much of its strength, it still remains a guiding force in many of the theories that are coming out.

The growth of the doctrine of evolution and that of the science of anthropology were on the parallel lines. "The doctrine of evolution and the science of anthropology did not spring upon the nineteenth century mind full-blown, like a dazzling intuition shattering all the previous fictions about man in a sudden intellectual sword-thrust. On the contrary, they were a result of cumulative process which derived its momentum from the vast movements of men and materials that had been set agog in that century. While theories of evolution, as we know, arose first with the Greeks, it was not until the eighteenth century, that they made any headway in the western world. The doctrine of evolution in the sociological fields had come, as would be apparent, from the biological fields – as a result of Darwinism.

Prior to Charles Darwin, in the works of such men as Buffon, Erasmus, Darwin, Goethe, Saint Hilaire and Lamarck, evolutionary hypothesis has been advanced in rapid succession. The very simultaneity with which Darwin and Wallace struck upon the theory of natural selection and the survival of the fittest was magnificent proof of the intense activity of the ideas at the same time. Every force in the environment, economic and social, conspired to the success of the doctrine.

If before 1859, Western civilization found its intellectual continuity in Biblical doctrine, after 1859, its found its new continuity in the doctrine of evolution. "A doctrine is only seized upon in that fashion, when it supplies some great need, emotional as well as intellectual, in the life of man. Darwin's theory of evolution supplied the need for a new philosophy of life. If not only afforded a new vista of human developments, but is also provided a new justification of world progress in terms of Western civilization. The entrance of this evolutionary creed into the sociological aroma was thus highly welcomed. People were waiting for some such explanation to account for the progress and were in the search of a clue to explain the "origin of civilization." The evolution of man was seen thus as a form of infinite progress, from lower forms to higher, modern civilization, and as representative of the highest form in the evolutionary scale. But more than that Darwin's theory of natural selection made survival synonymous with advance." Since all life was a 'struggle of the fittest' that which survived was the superior and the stronger one. The evolutionists had began to apply this in the field of natural sciences and argued that this process had survived the most successfully in the struggle of civilization, its much necessity represented the highest paid investment in thought.

Social Evolution

An idea of progress is inherent in almost all social institutions, and it is a tendency, usually, to discover for its causes, among the sociologists and other writers on the subject. Much nearer to this idea of progress there crept an idea of evolution among these writers, particularly of the last century – who began to discover - seek for the origin of all social institutions and all technology, and to treat development of civilizations, or the institutions in terms of continuous social process or evolution. Here thus lay the germs of a philosophy of social evolution, which in its full bloom came to command much influence during the last few decades.

The term "evolution", as we have referred, originally comes from biology, and is best defined in harmony with both its etymological and its biological meanings. Etymological to "evolve" is to "unroll or unfold": the evoling thing manifests traits that have until then been latent. In terms of biological sense, and according to Darwinian conception, evolution means "descent with modification."

As Lowie suggests, there is now general agreement that except in technological and purely intellectual phases of culture, "progress" cannot be objectively determined; hence it should not be tied up with a scientific principle, such as its evolution is supposed to be.

Unilinear and Multilinear Evolution

That social phenomena have evolved, i.e., derived from other social phenomena by a process of modification is a generally accepted proposition. It could not be otherwise for the matter is in one of observation and written record, in Lowie's, views. The present day political institutions are the "modified descendants of the past tribal-political groups, and that the present day caste-system evolved out of some former simple institution. While so far is the common agreement, scholars disagree concerning the course of evolution. Some believe that the course of evolution has been uniform, proceeding along more or less, same lines in all parts of the world, and that the peoples the world over have traversed the same stages of development. This is the theory of unilinear evolutionists. Other insist that evolution has been multilinear, travelling through different routes in diverse areas. They are ready to concede that though, there may have been a social evolution in the development of the various institutions in reaching their present form, it does not necessarily suggest that evolution may all along have been the same, or, along the same lines. They also admit that there may have been diverse conditions, social and others, which may have produced different results in different parts. It became a tendency with unilinear evolutionist to take a social institution or idea, and account for its origins. On the basis of their basic assumption they proceeded to think that it must be a later and modified form of some pre-existing social phenomena. They were the people much interested in the "reconstruction of the past." They tried to discover a causal relation for the present-day institutions and went to the remote past in their research to account for the present-phenomena through its fast antecedent. So far they were in common agreement with the multilinear evolutionists, for the interest, or aim of both was the same – the search for the evolution of our present day institutions – and to find an adequate explanation for all progress and civilization, that man has made since the dawn of his life on earth.

The difference occurs later in their methodology. The unilinear scholars can be said to be the 'extremists' – who had adopted an 'extreme' form of social evolution, while the multi-linearists took recourse to moderate form, making allowance for certain other factors of diversity in local conditions.

The theory of unilinear evolution is also conveniently referred to as "parallelism." This parallelism is typically represented in E.B. Tylor's famous statement: "The institutions of man are as distinctly stratified as the earth on which he lives. They succeed each other in series substantially uniform over the "globe", independent of what seem the comparative superficial differences of race and language, but shape by similar human nature, acting through successive changed conditions in savage, barbaric and civilized life. A concrete application of the parallelists principle is the once widespread view that all peoples with patrilineal clans previously reckoned descent through women."

The doctrine of social evolution gained its vigour and energy from an English author Lewis Henry Morgan. In the words of "Lowie" probably the most ambitious scheme of social evolution is that propounded by Lewis Morgan's *Ancient Society* with reference to family life and marriage. According to him, the several social and domestic institutions are to be understood as originating in the several branches of the human family, substantially in the order named, and as existing generally in these branches, while in the corresponding status.

He suggests a scheme or sequence of stages in the development of the present form of "monogamous" - marriage. These stages include promiscuity; the inter-marriage of brothers and sisters in a group; the inter-marriage of several sisters with one another's husbands; the clan organization barring sibling marriage; marriage of single pairs, but without exclusive cohabitation; monogamy. He declares that "progress has been substantially the same in kind in all tribes and nations inhabiting different and even disconnected continents; while in the same is status, with deviations form uniformity in particular instance, is produced by special causes.

At another place in *Ancient Society* : Morgan writes : "Modern institutions plant their roots in the period of barbarism, into which their germs were transmitted from the previous period of savagery. They have had a lineal descent, through ages, with the streams of the blood, as well as a logical development."

Morgan considers social evolution along two independent lines. The one leads through invention and discoveries, and the other through primary institutions. According to Morgan, the facts indicate the gradual formation and subsequent development of certain ideas, passions, and aspirations. Those which hold the most important positions may be generalized as growths of the particular ideas with which they severally stand connected. Apart from inventions and discoveries, they are the following : (i) subsistence, (ii) government, (iii) language, (iv) family, (v) religion, (vi) house, life and architecture, and (vii) property. Morgan considers each of these in his treatment of the social evolution.

Morgan traces the evolution of present civilization, through the periods of savagery and barbarism through which it must have passed before achieving its present form.

Thus he writes : "As it is undeniable that portions of the human family have existed in stage of savagery, portions in a state of barbarism, and still other portions in a state of civilization, it seems equally so that these three distinct conditions are connected with natural as well as the necessary sequence of progress. Moreover, that this sequence has been historically true of the entire human family, upto the status attained by each branch respectively, is rendered probable by the conditions under which all progress occurs, and by the known advancement of several branches of the family through two or more of these conditions."

Thus unilinear evolutionists got much inpetus from such contributions, and developed a theory of the nature of 'pigeon-whole' doctrine. The evolutionist of this school hastily drove upon any fact that fitted well into their own theory, they were blind to the other side of the question.

The believers in multilinear evolution do not form a single school. Some emphasize the uniqueness of historical events and would quote against parallelism, an earlier statement of Tylor : "Most of its (culture's) phenomena has grown into shape out of such a complication of events that the laborious piercing together of their previous history, is the only safe way of studying them." Others, notably the Austrian school headed by Father Schmidt, explain social evolution essentially in terms of a 'three fold' development. After a primeval period of hunting, they assume, man in one region perfected his hunting devices, and created certain crafts; elsewhere he domesticated wild animals species laying the foundation for pastoralism; in still another area he invented 'farming'. Each of these steps is supposed to have had repercussions in the social sphere. At subsequent periods, the three primary cultures entered into various relations, yield the range observable phenomena.

We find that among the multilinear evolutionists, Schmidt is not 'a whit' less of an evolutionist than Tylor. This appears both from explicit avowals of 'a belief in evolution' – and from the way in which he outlines the course of primary cultures. Still more clearly evolutionary theory of Schmidt is a theory of matriliny. Where the societies started with matriarchate, or with woman's superior powers in family and society.

Thus we find that theories of multinear evolution, in prescribing a fixed order assume a "law of sequence," just as much as do the unilinear systems. In both theories, specific causes bring about the alleged modifications.

These theories of evolution – both multilinear and unilinear forms – have been subject to criticism by the different writers. Some of the points of criticism are very basic. As all would agree, that it is only an abstruse – 'doctrinaire' philosophy to seek the same causes everywhere – leading to same effects, as is involved in the evolutionist's theory particularly of the unilinear type. Diversity of cultures and of physical and social conditions are the facts which should not be ignored in mind in the zeal for reconstruction of the past. Man is not the same everywhere in world. He differs essentially and largely in may ways. Then how institutions and technology and ideas could be the same everywhere ? Evolutionism by ignoring these basic facts, falls into "the jargon of dogmatism." And here lies the main flow in the evolutionary - doctrine.

Summing up, we can say, however, that parallelism is not to be ruled out, but the extent to which it operates is subject to criticism. It remains to be demonstrated by 'intensive' study.

Results to date suggest that "generalizations of limited validity are wholly possible. They also indicate the extreme improbability of a uniform sequence over long periods. Morgan's scheme for instance, implies an evolution extending over millennia. During such span of time there are bound to be so many "deviations from Uniformity" and – produced by special causes, that allow it to maintain an original uniform position.

2

Evolution of Marriage and Family

No Other Terms of anthropological significance are perhaps so much popular, common and easily understandable as 'marriage' and 'family'. Even one with little or no knowledge of anthropology understands what they mean. Marriage and family both are the results of social and biological necessities and can be understood only with reference to them.

What is Marriage?

Marriage has been defined as "the complex of social norms that define and control the relations of a mated pair to each other, their kinsmen, their offspring, and society at large." – (Hoebel).

It defines all the institutional demands, right duties, immunities, etc., of the pair of husband and wife. It is the institution that shapes the form and activities of the association known as the family.

Marriage implies mating, which is a "biological imperative deeply rooted in the sex drive and the need to reproduce." No human society can escape from the dictates of its imperative. By mating is meant "pairing off of individuals of opposite sex under the influence of the sexual drive." Mating implies more than sexual intercourse; a degree of performance is involved in the association of the mated pair. But marriage is not only mating. Mating occurs in other animals also. Mating is not to be confused with marriage, because, intimately connected though the two may be they are not inseparable. Thus inspite of the fact, that marriage meets basic biological needs, it is the 'social institution' determined.

As said above, marriage is the institution that shapes the form and activities of the association known as the family. Thus marriage is a social institution which unites the couple or pair under roof of a family, yet it can be conceded, that mating is the basic purpose of marriage, as Hoebel suggests.

E.W. Burgess, long an expert and scientific student of family, believes that "the sexual impulse itself is not sufficient to ensure more than the casual union of the sexes." Anthropological evidence, as we know, concurs in this point. Marriage fixes responsibility. Put another way, the function of marriage is "to make the world safe for family." Without marriage, the security of family would have been in danger.

Marriage is a culture complex. It is the characteristic behaviour as the members of the group of people who make up the family. This means, of course, that for descriptive purposes, marriage and the family are really one and the same, it is only for analytical reasons that we draw a distinction between them.

What is Family?

Family is a universal institution. As strictly defined, "Family is an association of husband and wife, and their offspring." It has also both sociological and biological bearings upon it. Biologically, as Lowie also points out, every community must rest on the family, the group comprising a married couple and their children. But biological and sociological necessity need not coincide. It does not follow that the biological family must exist as a unit differentiated from the rest of the social aggregate, of which it forms a part. Indeed, in such a stage of sexual communism as is pictured by Morgan's school, the family would be wholly submerged in a wider group. The matter is thus not one for a priori argument but empirical fact.

Family is the standard social unit today and it is found in some form or other in almost all levels of cultural development. Family is a group of persons who live under the same roof, are connected by blood and own a consciousness of kind on the basis of locality, interest and mutuality of obligations. "It is a defence unit as well as an aggressive one, and its performance is sanctioned by common property rights and residence under the same roof, as Majumdar suggests.

Family in a sociological sense, consisting of husband, wife and immature children, has existed in all phases of human cultural development, though side by side with the individual family, other forms were integrated or lose, have appeared and often the emphasis has been transferred from one to the other, without family disintegrating the original nucleus grouping.

In this sociological sense, family is characterised by two of its characteristic features – universality and – its bilateral character. as has been said, family is found universally, i.e., in every corner of the world, and in every society whether modern or primitive. Family recognises relationship from both the sides, from father's as well as mother's side. The family as a social unit includes both 'parents' and in a secondary sense, the kindred on both sides. Thus family is bilateral in character, as distinguished from clan which is unilateral.

Evolutionary Theory of Family and Marriage

The universality and supreme position of family has been challenged by some of the writers known as evolutionists in social anthropology. They suggested that family is not the oldest institution.

On the evolutionary principle, they attempted to suggest the development of family and marriage in terms of evolutionary process. As Lowie worthily remarks:

> When evolutionary principles, having gained general acceptance in biology, had begun to affect all philosophical thinking, it was natural to extend them to the sphere of social phenomena.

Morgan's Theory of Evolution of Family and Marriage

Among the first to embark on this venture was Lewis H. Morgan, an English by birth and lawyer by profession, whose ethnographical treatise on the Iroquois had established his reputation as an accurate and sympathetic observer of primitive custom.

Under the influence of evolutionary doctrines, Morgan outlined a complete scheme for the development of human marriage. Correlated with it goes the explanation of the development of family as it is found today in its present form.

Since the basic formulations of the evolutionary doctrine had been accepted, it was natural to seek for the hypothetical stages in the history of human society from where the present form of family may have evolved. Thus Morgan starts with 'agamy' – a time when there was no marriage – and complete indifference to sexual relations prevailed. This was the stage of primitive promiscuity according to Morgan.

There were no social laws or regulations in this period. It was eminently characteristic of the intellectual atmosphere of the period that Morgan' first stage should be a stage of primitive promiscuity, in which sexual lust was unrestricted by any incest rules. Complete lack of regulation of sex life is manifestly the diametrical opposite of obligatory monogamy, and the evolutionary theorist of the day was bent upon connecting the most diverse phenomena by a graded series of intermediaries. For the mid-Victorian thinker, to quote Lowie in this connection, "it was a foregone conclusion requiring only statement, not proof, that monogamy is the highest form of marriage in the best of conceivable universes; and it was equally axiomatic that early man must have lived under conditions 'infinitely' removed from that ideal goal." So, Morgan made no pretense at producing empirical proof or pristine promiscuity, which is fact, he assigned to the period when man was still hovering near the border line between humanity and a lower organic stage. He advanced promiscuity thus, as a 'logical postulate' – precisely as some evolutionary philosophers advance the axiom of spontaneous generation, and thereby placed it beyond the range of scientific discussion. This was the stage, in his opinion, when there was no family – as men had free and random to sexual practices, and did not establish any permanent bond.

The second stage of Morgan was of what he calls. 'Consanguine' or the Melayan family. This stage is based on the inter-marriage of brothers and sisters but barring that of parents and children. Here the group is promiscuous but with the limitation that only members of the same generation can inter-marry. This type of marriage is admitted to be 'a pure-deduction' from the classification system of polynesia, in which each membership is coterminous with the whole of its generation. The fact which Morgan adduced as conclusive proof of the former intermarriage of brothers and sisters was the Hawaiian method of designating kin. Morgan derived the evidence for this hypothetical stage – from the Hawaiian classificatory system – in which the kinship terms for "father" and "maternal uncle" are the same.

The next stage chalked in his scheme is that of consanguine-family. Morgan suggests that what is in common ethnographic parlance is called – "Group marriage", – viz., a condition in which "the group of men were conjointly married to the group of women." Morgan considers particularly the institution of several sisters sharing a group of husbands not necessarily kinsmen of one another and of several brothers sharing a group of wives, not necessarily related to one another. This sort of group-marriage is deduced from the relationship terms of the four-class system, in which people now marry their cross-cousins. Morgan assumed that the consanguine generation split into two, one of which contained brothers and sisters, and the other cross-cousins. This, in his view, father limited promiscuity.

The further development of marriage from group-marriage is in reaching to the present form of 'monogamy'. Morgan traces it through polygyny and polyandry, which are considered the two antecedants to monogamy. The next step from group marriage is of the "non-fraternal polyandry" – from where it passed to fraternal or adelphic type of polyandry. The next-stage after polyandry, postulated by Morgan is that of voluntary management which passed later into polygyny. The next and last stage – after this – is monogamy- (enforced) in which the human societies are living today. This scheme of the evolution of family and marriage, as suggested by Morgan, can be represented in this way :

From Agamy or the stage of primitive promiscuity —>Consanguine-Family —>Group marriage, —>Non-Fraternal polyandry —>Fraternal polyandry —>Voluntary Monogamy —>Polygyny —>Monogamy (Enforced) or to express in other words, if we put the promiscuous-stage at the bottom as the foundation of the structure, the monogamy (in its present form) would be at the summit of edifice – while the other forms of consanguine-family, group-marriage, polyandry and polygyny – would form the intermediaries or in-between steps.

This was the evolutionary scheme of marriage and family as expounded by Morgan in his *Ancient Societies*.

McLennan's View

Besides, the other writers have also suggested the evolution of marriage and family from some primeval level.

A contemporary to Morgan, McLennan, attempted to explain the evolution and development of family – in his *Primitive Marriage* – (Edinburgh, 1865) and reprinted in *Ancient History* (1876).

He was also nearly to the same idea of a succession of primitive promiscuity, mother-right, or exogamy leading to father-right and father-right based however on wholly different inductions. In the beginning was a stage of sexual indifference, or primitive promiscuity, during which, there existed homogeneous "stock-groups" without any organized forms of marriage.

For him, totemism is prior to exogamy, for exogamy does not begin until his second stage, when a scarcity of women causes marriage by capture on apparent survivals of such practice, first gave McLennan – the idea of the investigating the history – of the family. While Maine confined his investigation to one type of people, and based his arguments almost entirely on Roman Law, McLennan made a wider induction – from a number of primitive peoples. But he assumed too much or too little evidence.

Thus McLennan's theory is also vitiated by almost the common defects of the evolutionary doctrines.

Lubbock's View

The period of Morgan and McLennan was one in which it was almost a fashion to talk of evolution and seek to attempt to account for it in one way or the other.

Sir John Lubbock considered the evolution of family in 1870 in *The Origin of Civilization* dealing besides with arts and ornaments, religion, law, language and morals. He has defined marriage as "an exclusive relation of one or more men with one or more women, based on custom, recognized and supported by public opinion, and where law exists, by law, "and considers that such marriage was preceded by a previous stage of what he calls – "communal marriage." This was a stage, according to him in which all the men and women in a small community were regarded as equally married to each other. It is from such a stage that Lubbock traces the evolution of family, as it is in its present form. With McLennan, he agrees that the change from communal to individual marriage occurred when marriage by capture started. They were encouraged since they were more exclusive, affectionate, convenient and productive of sound healthy children. Thus, in his own view, by degrees, exogamy became the rule; while Mclennan defined 'exogamy' – as the rule by which, the union of persons of the same social group is regarded as 'incest', as distinct from 'endogamy' which is 'the rule' by which the members of a group are forbidden to intermarry with members of another group, which are free to marry among themselves.

Westermarck's Views

It was however Westermarck to raise the voice against all those evolutionary schemes. He had dealt a fatal blow to these evolutionists by his well-known, celebrated work, *The History of Human Marriage* published in 1891.

He has defined marriage therein as a more or less durable connection of male and female lasting till and after the birth of the offspring.

He also severally challenged those who had disputed the existence of family in the early period of human society, and made it a strong point, that human family had existed since the very dawn of man's life on the earth. He also emphasized that man was since ever monogamous and never promiscuous, and he proved this by the evidence from apes.

It was Westermarck first thus, to claim, the universality and priority of family, fighting against all evolutionary schemes advanced by Morgan and others. Westermarck believed that monogamous family has existed in all levels of society and even some of the birds and animals are monogamous, while others have found polygyny side by side with monogamy and incest as the exception rather than a rule.

Westermarck's notable contribution was in the fact, that it had shaken the evolutionary claim by attacking at its very roots.

An Evolution of the General Views

The evolution of family-life and marriage had been traced by different writers in their own ways. Baschofen and others traced matriarchy from group-marriage and patriarchy has been claimed to have established itself due to male personality development or from a consideration of property. Morgan traced the evolution of family from a stage of primitive promiscuity and Marx and Engels developed the theory of origin of family on the basis of historical materialism, as the 'reflex of socio-economic relations of man'. They believe that each social aspect of man's production determines the form of family, and they have castigated the marital code of today and the ideal of monogamy as unnatural and bourgeoisic. Westermarck, as we have shown, had believed that monogamous family has existed in all levels of society and apes and even some of the birds and animals are monogamous and that polygyny, if in some cases, is found as exception rather than a rule. Some anthropologists have challenged the validity of Westermarck's contention about the extent and priority of family – and have discarded it as 'rationalization', and effort to differentiate man from the animal, ennobling the former at the expense of the latter, an effort to establish the culture of man, his distinctiveness and remoteness from the animal.

Malinowski has in a way accepted Westermarck's position and distinguished man from animals, on the ground that among primates, there is a ruthing season which is absent in man, indicating a difference in kind between man and animal.

Malinowski has maintained in his treatise *Sex and Repression in Savage Society*, that the family is the only type of grouping that man has carried over from the animal stage and he even denies the possible existence or sexual promiscuity; for gregarious tendency, according to him, was not the root of human organization. As Majumdar remarks : "If the biological postulate on which such generalizations are based, is found to be wanting, the whole superstructure of moral ideas of Westermarck falls to the ground."

It should be noted here that the extreme claims of Morgan, Marx and Engels, who trace the origin of family form sexual communism through stages and from a system of social production, seldom find corroboration from ethnographic evidence, though, their arguments may appeal to a class ridden society with opposing interests. Just as the discovery of monogamy among savages does not prove its universality, the presence of license and sexual lapses in savage society does not conform promiscuity as an initial stage. But both Morgan's and Westermarck's theories survive today, not because they are true, but because the theories are based on a dynamical concept of the family. The theories are substantiated today, not because they are accepted by the social sciences, but because the close interests are so hostile to each other that in the context of such hostility and antagonism, both the interpretations hold partial key to the social situation created by the productive technique of the day.

An Evaluation of Morgan's Contribution

Having discussed a general evaluation of the views with regard to the evolution of family and marriage, let us revert again to morgan's contribution in this field, and examine critically to what degree it has been of significance in suggesting some fundamental ideas, of evolutionary doctrines.

The historical stages in Morgan scheme of evolution and development of marriage, have been termed the "Sexual Communism." Some light on Morgan's basic formulation is shed by Lowie's remark, as he calls it the "Hypothetical Sexual Communism".

Morgan had started his scheme of evolutionary theory of marriage and family in a period when it was almost a fashion of the day. In that mid-Victorian age, monogamy was hailed as the highest form of marriage in the best of conceivable universes and, therefore, Morgan was led to put it as the ideal and at the height of the evolutionary scale. Now to explain a grading of scales in evolution before reaching that high goal, it was natural for the mid-Victorian thinker to start from some lower or sub-human period of civilization. Hence, Morgan made primitive promiscuity – which was conceived by him as the diametrical opposite of monogamy – the logical postulate of his evolutionary scheme. And the evolutionary theorist was bent upon connecting the most diverse phenomena by a graded series of intermediaries – which he suggested in other forms of marriages, such as group marriage, polyandry and polygyny. Secondly, we find that the very foundation on which Morgan built his logical postulate was wrong. We find that Morgan had derived his evidence for promiscuity – and group-marriage and consanguine-family from the Polynesian or Hawaiian data. While he was building his theory of evolutionary scheme, he drove upon the Hawaiian kinship terminologies and finding that while many primitive peoples carefully distinguished between maternal and paternal relatives, the Hawaiian not only drew no such distinctions – but apply their kinship terms, so as to include all relatives of the same generation, regardless of propinquity. For example, the term 'makua' there designates both the parents and all their brothers and sisters, sex being indicated by qualifying words – meaning 'man' and 'woman', Morgan argues that the maternal uncles were called by the same term as the fathers because all 'were fathers in the sense of having free access to their sisters; that similarly all of a man's nephews and nieces were called sons and daughters because all his sisters were his wives, as they were the wives of his brothers; and so forth. It is Morgan's contention that while the customs reflected in kinship nomenclature have a tendency to pass out of existence terminology itself is more conservative and thus furnished a sort of palaeontological record of social institutions. The really fundamental error, however, lies in Morgan assumption that a native term translated father is synonymous in the native mind with 'procreator'. Thus we find that the defect with Morgan lies in reading "unwarranted meanings in the polynesian data – rather a defect in the disease of thought.

It would really be a grave error to apply the meanings which are indeed unwarranted. The fact is that the Hawaiians have a common term for father and maternal uncle which is equivalent to the procreator but this does not in any case imply that maternal uncle may at some time have been the begettor. To conclude so, would be to mistake the evidence. In English, there may not be a common term strictly corresponding to that of the Hawaiians.

In short, we find that Morgan fails to prove that the Hawaiians must have had its origin in the inter-marriage of brothers and sisters, and even if it had arisen in this fashion there would be no proof that either the terminology or its hypothetical cause is of great antiquity.

Thus we find that Morgan's argument for the consanguine family based on such hypothetical evidence falls to the ground.

Morgan's second argument is that for the "group-marriage , viz., a condition in which the "group of men were conjointly married to the group of woman." Morgan, we find considers particularly the institution of several sisters, sharing a group of husbands and not necessarily kinsmen of one another; and several brothers sharing a group of wives not necessarily related to one anther. Group-marriage might, of course, be conceived, somewhat differently, though always involving a combination of polyandry with polygyny.

It is true that Morgan interpreted the sororate as a relic of group marriage, and Frazer has extended the phrase to the levirate as well. But these are empty guesses which may be disregarded. Levirate and Sororate are real institutions, intelligible only in their context; they are not rendered one whit more intelligible by conceiving them as survivals of conditions – that have never been observed.

Summing up this issue, we can say that sexual communism - as a condition taking the place of the individual family exists nowhere at the present time; and the arguments for its former existence must be rejected as unsatisfactory – while they are still subjected to hot controversy.

Morgan, as we have noted somewhere in course of our discussion, had also argued for the priority of sib or clan over the family. In his opinion, clan was older and fundamental than the family – which is rather a late product. We find here that this theory for the priority of clan – over family – is also based upon - Morgan's main postulate of promiscuity – in which complete inbreeding prevailed, which resulted in the deterioration of the stock, and since men became conscious of this fact, they attempted to check it. Hence, "Sibs arose because of a remarkable reformatory movement, that retrenched inter-marriage of blood-relations, gained a foothold, through biologically beneficial result thereby and spread its consequence over an enormous area.

But this view of the priority of clan – over the family has been severally challenged by the later writers. As we have seen

Westermarck had dealt a fatal blow to Morgan's conception of primitive promiscuity and group marriage. In a similar manner, he demolished his theory of the priority of sib. He showed by means of ethnographic evidence, that family as a universal social institution has been existing since all times and in all conditions - and that sib is only a late product.

After him, Lowie has also criticised Morgan's dispute over the priority of family.

"The bilateral family is an absolutely universal institution", – writes Lowie, "on the other hand, the unilateral sib has only a restricted though wide distribution." It is true that many of the more highly civilized nations of the world, like the Greeks, are known to have passed through a period in which they were organized into sibs. But this may simply indicate that at a certain level, the sib system tends to decay, leaving the always co-existing family in possession of the field, it does not by any means prove that the sib is older than the family. A survey of the data clearly shows that the family is omnipresent at every stage of culture; that at a higher level it is frequently coupled with a sib organization; and that at a still higher level the sib disappears.

This simple statement of fact, however, runs counter to one of the most generally accepted and least warrantable of Morgan's speculations. For Morgan held that family was late product which had been almost uniformly preceded by the sib. But as we have seen above this argument for the priority of sib as advanced by Morgan, does not stand group in the light of later criticisms raised against it.

"Reviewing the whole case for the evolution of family and marriage – as suggested by the evolutionary theorists and as we have examined above, though highly suggestive of some evolutionary process in the development of social institutions – and in suggesting the dynamicity of the family-life, is valuable, yet it does not corroborate with the factual evidence and as put forward by its enthusiast propounder it becomes an exaggerated picture of human-history.

Marriage and family have been known to man – since hunger and thirst and they have become rather a part and parcel of his social life. they will continue to have their social value for him – so far man realises the need of social – life.

3

The Contribution of Tylor to Early Social Anthropology

A Great Name to be recognised towards the end of the last century was that of Edward Burnett Tylor (1832-1917). Tylor has contributed much to the science of man, both in quality and quantity of its material; his contribution in one way that of covering a larger field of subjects, often surpasses that of his other contemporaries.

Tylor belongs to what has been called, the Heroic period of British Civilization. It is said about him that, "none represented British anthropology more worthily than Tylor."

Tylor had started his early career under Christy, by whom he was much influenced in his life. Christy was a pre-historic archaeologist. It was in his company that Tylor went to Mexico in 1836. He worked with Christy there for a considerably long time. After coming back from there he wrote some papers. Since then he devoted himself much to the study of primitive life, though not on field. In 1896, he became the Professor of Anthropology at Oxford.

Though technically, he was not a field-worker in the sense of a true anthropologist, like Morgan, he was also none of the armchair theorists.

Tylor's main contribution lies in the fields of religion, culture and social institutions (which includes his rules of residence). He wrote three main works :

1. Researches into the Early History of Mankind and the Development of Civilization.
2. Two volumes on Primitive Culture, and
3. A popular text-book on – Anthropology in two volumes.

He is much known for furthering the concept of culture, and still more for introducing behind it the idea of 'diffusion'. The purpose of the present essay is only to examine his contributions in all the above-noted fields.

Rules of Residence

In his paper – 'On a method of investigating the Development of Institutions, applied to the Laws of Marriage and Descent', Tylor showed how the development of institutions might be examined with the help of tabulation and classification. Taking data from all over the world, he arranged in tables the rules of marriage and descent, together with the "adhesion" of each system, "showing which peoples have the same customs, and what other customs accompany it or lie apart from it. For example, the rules of residence after marriage with the wife's people, with the husband's people, or beginning with the wife's and ending with the husband's people, were compared by him with the adhering customs of a man's avoidance of his wife's parents, or of a woman's avoidance of her husband's. Thus Tylor furnished his theory regarding the Rules of Residence, and supported it by the practical illustrations picked up from different societies.

The rules of residence after marriage are likewise discussed in connection with 'Teknonymy', i.e., the naming of parents after children, with the 'levirate', 'couvade' and 'marriage by capture'. The evidence drawn on the basis of all these facts, as far as it goes, appears to show that the residence with the wife's people is anterior to the residence of the wife with the husband's. Thus Tylor's attempt in giving out these rules of residence, was only to point out that matrilocal residence preceded patrilocal.

Matriarchal Theory

Tylor also posits the priority of matriarchy over patriarchy on a number of grounds. To him, society has passed from matriarchy to patriarchy. For proving this he takes the resort of geological evidences. He believed that fossil finds of the geological strata furnish sufficient evidence for such a belief. Taking help of the statistical method, in his search for geological evidences, he succeeded in laying out his complete scheme. Being a social evolutionist, Tylor believed in the gradual stages in the development of society. He recoursed himself with the archaeological layer of the fossils, and came in touch with the statistical method. He found the fossil-evidences for customs, such as couvade and avunculate in the first stage, but which were found to be absent in the second or later stage. On the basis of this, he inferred that matriarchy may have preceded patriarchy.

Tylor stretches the same theory to account for the priority of matrilineal sibs over patrilineal ones. The error with Tylor, as we notice on a thorough examination of his views, lies not in his hypothesis of the priority of matriarchy, matrilocal residence, or matrilineal sibs, over patriarchy, patrilocal residence and patrilineal sibs, but with his unilineal attempt to explain the development of all societies all over the world, from a single inherent cause. And it is here that Tylor errs.

It is well-nigh possible that some societies may have ever since been patrilocal and patrilineal. One single principle cannot be found to operate in case of all societies. This fact should have been taken note of, by Tylor, but which, he unfortunately either missed, or ignored. There seems the possibility of a parallel development of patrilineal and matrilineal societies. In case of the Nagas and the Khasis of Assam, we find that though they live quite near to each other, they are quite different to each other in their social structure. The former are patrilineal, while the later have a matrilineal system. This gives strength rather to the parallel development than to an unilineal one.

We find that Tylor errs in another respect also. While drawing inferences on the basis of the evidence collected by him, he ignores the functional role altogether. He neglects the function of a particular system in relation to its total social structure, and eagerly takes out facts to fit well into his scheme. In his eagerness to prove that matriarchal societies preceded patriarchal ones, he proceeded by defining three stages:

1. In the maternal type – matrilineal descent is coupled with avuncular authority and nepotic inheritance.
2. At the opposite pole, patriarchal society has patrilineal descent, patriarchal authority and filial succession.
3. In the intermediary type, features of the two are invariably blended.

Here he used the argument of archaeology of fossil remains in the shape of survivals. Couvade must have been absent in the matrineal stage, twenty times in the transitional stage, and eight times in the patrilineal stage.

Thus we find that though, Tylor's explanation seems to be based on logical grounds, with the knowledge of geological evidences, it cannot be accepted as the only valid explanation. If social evolution is to be accepted or any rate as historical or fact, multilineal scheme would definitely be more scientific and admissible than the unilineal. Yet it also remains a fact to remember, that Tylor was far from being an unilinear evolutionist with a simple and unilineal scheme of development, and at many places, he refuses to go beyond data to mere speculation. At one place, he also remarks:

> It is not meant to imply, that the maternal-family as here set forth, represents the primitive condition of mankind, but that it is a stage through which the inhabitants of a greater part of the world, now in the paternal stage, appear to have passed, and which still continues in force over considerable part of the globe, except Europe.

Classificatory System and Exogamy

Tylor has also dealt with Exogamy, and the "Classificatory System" of relationship. In his view, "Exogamy and Classificatory System" of relationship are two sides of the same 'system' – which binds together a whole community with ties of kinship and affinity. The classificatory system expresses the relationship between all the members of a clan, that is, of people who are descended from a common-ancestor, or believe themselves to be so descended, or feel their unity and express it by some common symbol, such as a totem. The rule of exogamy requires the members of a group to marry the members of another particular group or groups. Within the tribe, and keeps the growing tribal compact. Such marriages often result in the almost complete endogamy of the tribe, the relationship system emphasizing the solidarity of the different clans and the system of marriage preserving the solidarity of the tribe.

Theory of Culture Diffusionism

Tylor gets much credit for his theory of culture. He is associated with the theory of "diffusion of culture". Diffusionism holds that a particular part of culture (or a culture-object) can be invented only at one place, from where it spreads to other parts of the world, and is thus 'diffused'. Thus for example, according to the diffusionist theory of culture, potter's wheel which is in use in many part of the world today, must have been invented at one particular place, from where it must have gradually passed on to other places. Hence diffusion might have taken place. This was the original and simple form of the diffusionist theory, in which it was originated. Later on, this diffusionist theory became more complex in its form as well as in its implications, as its beliefs stretched it further and further, according to their own views. Thus it was developed to include the difficult enquiry regarding the invention, borrowing and diffusion of culture, culture-traits and culture-elements all over the world. In America this school not only made considerable progress, but could be counted as a force and is, in fact, pre-dominant even today. "In England, the enthusiast adherents of this school threw all moderation to winds and elaborated such fantastic theories that within a limited time, diffusionism of this (extreme) variety stood exposed and self-condemned." – as S.C. Dubey has pointed out. And this was the diffusionism as seen and interpreted by Eliot Smith. Eliot Smith, the chief exponent of this school, in his enthusiasm went further, so as to look towards Egypt as the seat of all civilization and the centre of all diffusion. To him, man was very uninventive, and the very exceptional conditions for the development of culture existed only in Egypt. And all civilization spread from Egypt to the rest of the world. Yet such fanaticism was not involved in Tylor's diffusionism – as he understood and interpreted it. It was all simple in nature and clear in its implications. His diffusionism had the outstanding merit in as much as it also made allowance to admit the role of parallelism, where it might be necessary. Being a pre-historian also, Tylor could determine the role that diffusionism may have played into some parts of the world. He was, however, alive to the fact, that for social institutions, diffusionism alone cannot always be the explanation. Though Tylor was always producing some or the other argument to explain culture-contact in order to support diffusionism, he was wise enough to admit, before being landed into severe criticism, that both diffusionism and parallelism may have been at work in different places.

We can ascertain his position in this connection, in a remark which he himself made once. "The facts collected seem to favour the view that the wide differences in the civilization and mental states of various races of mankind are rather "difference of development, than of origin, rather of degree than of kind." He was, however, extremely careful, not to admit the independent origin of similar inventions in different parts of the world, until he had exhausted every possibility of diffusion or culture-contact.

So much has been written of late years to the effect that Tylor was a simple unilinear evolutionist who tore in a developmental scheme with little regard to their function in their own culture, that it is perhaps excusable to point out that all through his career, it is evident, that like Darwin and Bastion, he kept the whole complex of life with its interdependence of view. But at the same time it should also be reckoned that – Tylor was fully alive to the necessity for examining the function of any particular institution within its own culture before using it in a developmental scheme. He shows that totems have different functions in different places, and are differently conceived by different peoples. In his view, the consideration of the functions of totemism in various parts of the world, makes it impossible to say – much more than animal–worship, and the idea of some connection between groups of man and species of animals are characteristic of many peoples in lower grades of civilization. While allowing full credit to the necessity for studying diffusion and function, Tylor held, like Bastion, to the idea of the Psychic Unity of mankind.

Resemblances and Differences

Tylor has also discussed certain other social facts. He suggests that in different parts of the world, many similarities and differences, are found. How are they to be accounted for ? He pointed out that various explanations put forward to explain these, in fact, fail to do so. As for the resemblances, Tylor recognised two things:

1. Some inherent law for all human kind, and
2. Diffusionism.

Tylor refuted the geographic explanation put forward by Ratzel, that geography is the main determining factor, and maintained strongly that geography can at best lay down the negative limits, but it can in no way be the determining factor.

Tylor's greatest contribution, however, was the study of primitive religion, besides his study of social organization and law. No one before him had tried to analyse and lay down in such precise terms the definition and meaning of religion. Tylor had that zeal to attempt it, and also to succeed in it to a great length.

Tylor attempted to lay down the minimum definition of religion in the following words: "Religion is a belief in spiritual beings." He was the first to revive the view that there were tribes without religion, and suggested the Universality of religion, just as Westermarck had suggested the universality of family. In this connection he wrote: "the asserted existence of non-religious tribes in question, rests on an evidence often mistaken and never conclusive. He was also responsible for separating the dross from the gold, and thus "rescued the substantive body of authentic knowledge.

No sooner his Primitive culture had appeared in 1871, Tylor became widely known as the "foremost" of the British anthropologists. For the next thirty years, there was hardly any other theory to hold the field there, or in America, or on the continent.

Animism

Tylor found the essence of religion in "Animism" that is a "belief in Spiritual Beings". And because such belief had been reported from all adequately described tribes on the face of the globe. Tylor inferred the universality of religion. Tylor found that most of the primitive tribes of the world foster a belief in some or the other ways in the animistic nature of religion. The currency to the term Animism was given by Tylor himself. His scheme of the treatment of animism naturally divides itself into two parts:

1. His account of the origin of Spirit concept: In this he determines how the concept of comparatively spiritual as opposed to grossly material existence could ever have arisen.
2. His theory of Nature and sequence of Supernatural Beings: Under this, he attempts to show, when that concept had once evolved, all types of Supernatural Beings evolved from it.

Tylor has called Animism the philosophy of the soul. Tylor believed that all primitive people believe in soul. They regard some part of the body as the seat of the soul: some regard blood, some heart and others liver as the seat of the soul. Tylor suggests, that man came to have the idea of soul, from his dream experiences, when he found that the soul leaves the body. Man sees shadows and he tries to catch them, but he cannot. He thinks that it is something which he cannot catch and develops the idea of a double. His reflection in tanks, his echoes in forests, the dreams he sees, all help him, according to Tylor, in developing the idea of the double. These things are elusive and the primitive man tried to grapple with these ideas. Tylor says that such experiences helped him to develop the philosophy of double'. He thought that this double can leave the body temporarily as it does in dreams, and return again to it when the man awaken and primitive people thus believe in spirits also and want to please them. The spirit is recognised as evil and the primitive man tries to please it and keep it off. This gives rise to Animism.

Thus Tylor tried to show the origin of religion from animism, or a belief in spiritual beings.

A Critical Appreciation of Tylor's Theory or Religion

Tylor's scheme of Animistic religion has been severally criticized by the French sociologist, Durkheim. Durkheim attacked Tylor's theory on many points, as he pointed towards many discrepancies involved in it.

The French sociologist raises severe objections to Tylor's theory of religion, as he asks – "Why should a primitive man crave a theoretical interpretation of dream-life? He is not a philosopher who deliberately concocts theories of the phenomena observed." Durkheim contends that the dream phenomena are not most simply explained by the assumption of a double; for example, it would have been simpler for a dreamer to imagine himself with the telescopic vision, when he sees remote regions in his sleep.

But Durkheim is himself willing to grant that nowadays the savage uses the concept of the double to account for dream apparitions, but he maintains that this represents a later stage of development. He argues that primitive man does not explain all dreams alike, but disregards the majority of them; he pays more attention only in so far they are sanctified by a pre-existing religious system.

Durkheim is not more fortunate when he argues that our dreams very often relate to past experiences, that we survey once more what we have already seen, do again what we have done. All thus he insists cannot be explained by the double. Durkheim assumes that the most archaic religious conceptions are those found in Australia.

But, as Lowie has tried to defend the position of Tylor in the following comment: "It is undoubtedly true that Tylor's phraseology is often tinctured with rationalistic psychologising, but Durkheim does not put his finger on the right spot. Tylor is in fault so far as he limits the consideration of religion almost wholly to the beliefs in the spiritual beings, that is, to the conceptual aspect of religion, without due regard to its emotional concommitants. But in the present context, the charge of intellectualism is pointless, because Tylor is concerned with tracing the origin of a concept, that is, to a cognitive element of consciousness. Further, he derives it very largely not from ratiocination about observed phenomena, but from the immediate sensory, testimony of dream-life." But, as Lowie has also pointed out, Durkheim's objections leave Tylor's explanation entirely unshaken. Certainly, the alternative proposed by the critic cannot be regarded as an adequate substitute.

Tylor's formation is not exacting enough, for it omits an essential determinant of the phenomena to be defined. Yet, we can agree with Lowie, that his theory is avowedly a psychological interpretation, pure and simple, but in as much as it not only explains the empirical observations, but operates exclusively with facts, like dreams, vision and the mortal end, all of which demonstrably exercise a strong influence on the minds of primitive men, it must be conceded to have a high degree of probability.

Reverting to that problem that engaged Tylor's attention, it can be said: Religion is a universal feature of human culture, not because all societies foster a belief in spirits, but because, all recognise in some form or other, the aweinspiring, extraordinary manifestations of reality. Owing to many ramifications of such supernaturalism, this definition does not lead to a rigid exclusion, but, merely to a somewhat different appraisal of features, commonly treated under the head of religion.

Still, we find, that Tylor's contribution made in this field, is not without value. His theory of religion, with a belief in spiritual being at its base, may not seem tangible to many of his critics, but its importance in as far as giving a minimum definition of religion, is something which can also not be easily ignored. As Penniman has so nicely remarked in this context: "His solidarray of accurately attested facts, his common-sense in interpreting them, and the beautiful simplicity of his style in dealing with so vast an amount of evidence – a style and power akin to Darwin, was immediate recognition for his views, and gave them a permanent place in the history of religion. It is his discovery of Animism and his ideas about witchcraft, magic and spiritualism that exercise a great influence all over the post-theories of religion, whatsoever.

"From survivals in games, proverbs, riddles and minor superstitions, such as those of sneezing, Mr Tylor glides into Magic as based on the association of ideas, into omens, automatism, witchcraft and spiritualism and the doctrine of Spirits, Animism with religion and mythology" as Andrew Lang had made a remark in his Preface to the "Essay Presented to Tylor (1907)".

Their Characteristic Contributions

Besides the above contributions made by the great British anthropologist of the nineteenth century in the fields of culture, religion and social organization, that there are some other characteristics with Tylor, which distinguished him from his other contemporaries. One such characteristic with him was his inclusiveness of all aspects of culture and society in dealing with the subject. By that time it was a common practice among the anthropologists or those interested in the subjects to confine themselves to only one sphere. Most of his contemporaries and successors, like Frazer, Andrew Lang, and Marret confined their researches to one or the other aspects, viz., religion, culture, or social institutions." W.H.R. Rivers confined himself to social organization, while Pitt-Rivers and A.C. Haddan to technology and primitive art only. Tylor was unlike all these contemporary writers, and he tried to embrace the whole field of anthropology, though he could not contribute equally to all those fields, as he had wished. Besides dealing with a number of things, such as culture, social organization, law and religion, he also engaged himself in the study of linguistics or comparative philology.

Another thing which characterizes Tylor is his selectiveness of data. He had uncanning resources. In his time much of the globe was not known ethnographically, and the reports that were coming were often mingled with fancies and myths. Tylor had the neck of selecting the worthy and rejecting the unworthy material.

Tylor's theories are supported by scientific evidences. His conclusions are based more on truth than on imagination. To those who would criticise a new subject, he claims that,"anthropology simplifies the acquisition and understanding of knowledge by showing the simple fundamentals of all human practices, enabling us to disentangle the mystifying growth that have come with later ages."

Conclusion

Concluding Tylor's contribution to the science of man, we may mention that the advent of Edward B. Tylor in British anthropology was an event of unique significance to the science of man. He was no field-worker. His experience of tribes was extremely limited, for he visited tribal areas only twice, once in the beginning of his scientific-career, he accompanied a pre-historian to Maxico (as noted above), and later as Professor at Oxford he visited the Pueblo Indians for a short while. In his writings many anthropological concepts assumed an added clarity. His definitions of religion and culture, and his emphasis on some fact of social organization, such as local exogamy, teknonymy and cross-cousin marriage lead to considerable clarification of thought on these issues. His systematization of available evidence pointed out to the many lamentable gaps in the existing knowledge of anthropology. Almost as a direct consequence there was increased field-activity and more and more attention was given to the problems of methodology.

In the light of these facts the importance of the contribution made by Tylor cannot be underestimated.

4

Morgan's Early Anthropological Thoughts

IT Is Only of recent past that the emphasis on field work in anthropology is being stressed much and for a scientific study of the subject.

The time when Morgan had become interested in the study of primitive peoples, little of field-work was known and much of anthropology by that time was only of the nature of arm-chair philosophy.

English by birth and lawyer by profession, Lewis Morgan (1818-81) had become interested in the subject towards the middle of his life, which was some time in the fifties of the last century. With the publication of his *Ancient Society* in 1877, he at once became famous, "not because of any solid work or research, but because of an historical accident." His *Ancient Society* had attracted the attention of Marx and Engels, who were in the search for such material which could tally with their own ideas about the historical past of the subject, and which Morgan had readily brought forth in the *Ancient Society.* Thus they welcomed Morgan's efforts, in drawing, on the basis of his hypotheses, a picture of the past which much tallied with the picture they themselves had in their own minds. And thus within a very short period following the publication of his work, Morgan was known the world over, and got the honour of first rate anthropologist and celebratee.

Morgan's major contribution to the science of anthropology lies in the field of "classificatory system of nomenclature." In fact, it was Morgan himself who discovered the Dakota-type of nomenclature and solved its usage and importance. By the material so valuable, furnished by the discoverer, it now forms a main aspect in the study of primitive societies.

Morgan divided the Kinship system into two types – the Classificatory and the Descriptive.

Among many peoples it is an assumption that all who live together make up the home circle and are related to each other, and it is considered that other groups are also related in the same way among themselves. Morgan pointed out that if the man stay at home and the wives come from outside, all the men of one's generation will be called by some term – which means "brother", and all the women by some term which means "sister". One's own father, his brothers and cousins, and even more remotely related men of his generation will be called by a term – which means "father". And same will be the case with the other side of the family, the mother, her sisters, cousins on her side and so on will be "mothers". This Morgan termed as the "Classificatory-System" of kinship. Thus in a classificatory or Dakota-type of kinship terminology, a specific term may be used for a set of persons in relation, including sometimes, even too remote ones to be so recognised. The simplest and most highly developed form of such classificatory system of Kinship is furnished by the people in a Maori village, where all the grandparent's generation are grand-parents, and of the father's or mother's generation are fathers or mother's, all of one's own are brothers and sisters, and all of one's own generation are referred to as "my children".

There are various forms of classification in different parts of the world, but in all the classificatory system expresses the extreme solidarity of the group and the mutual privileges and obligations of the group. To quote a few examples, among the 'Santhals', father's sister's husband, mother's brother, father-in law (both male speaking and female speaking) all have a common kinship term "Hoyan". Similarly in the Tamilian society, mother's brother, father's sister's – husband and father-in-law, all are addressed by the same kinship term – "Mama", because of cross-cousin-marriage. Again, the Sema-Nagas have a specific term of kinship – "Angu" to address a number of persons, viz. , mother's brother, mother's brother's children (son or daughter, both), husband's father (female speaking), wife's father (male speaking), husband's brother (female speaking) and wife's brother (male speaking).

A man's status is determined by his birth into such a group, an he has duties and privileges, with regard to every other member of the group. In societies which have no such system, (such as the Western society), Morgan pointed out, contract largely takes the place of status; members of families or social groups need have no concern for each other, and "the dole takes the place of mutual aid." Such a system, where our forms of address do not classify any relation but are merely "descriptive", Morgan called the Descriptive System of kinship.

Morgan had worked intensively among the Red Indian tribes from where he had collected much of his data. As early as 1846, while collecting material to illustrate the institutions of Iraquois, Morgan had found among them, "a system relationship for the designation and classification of kindred, both unique and extra-ordinary in its character, and wholly unlike any with which we are familiar. Morgan went still further collecting his data of classificatory systems in different parts of the world, so that at length he was able to present and analyse in all, 139 systems.

"Morgan had very rightly assumed that social reasons were at the root of the system, which he discovered, but unfortunately in *Ancient Society* 1877, he passed over a magnificent opportunity to relate these terms to active and observable social causes, and proceeded, like the other unilinear evolutionists, to develop the family by a typological series of forms, some of them purely hypothetical", as Penniman points out in his *A Hundred Years of Anthropology*.

Morgan with his theory of classificatory system went further to believe that the kinship terminologies cannot be borrowed, and where similarity between any two or more such kinship systems is found, it only points out the migration of people from one place to another. On the basis of this assumption he pointed out, though only hypothetically and not very scientifically, that in case of the Tamilian tribes of South India and Iroquo tribes of New York, among whom there is much similarity in the kinship system, Tamilians might have migrated to New York. Thus at one place, Morgan writes : "When the discoverers of the New World bestowed upon the native inhabitants the name of Indians, under the suspicion that they had reached Indians, they little suspected that the children of the same original family, although of a different continent were the same. By a single coincidence, the error was a truth."

This, however, seems fantastic, and Lubbock called it a "mystic nonsense", and demolished the whole of his theory by severe criticism.

We find, thus, that where Morgan had the amazing capacity to draw inferences and follow conclusions from them, he lacked the historic sense which is so essential for a fair and scientific treatment of any theory. Thus the grave charge that his critics are prone to level against him, is that he was very haste in drawing conclusions from his inferences and did not venture to take into account sufficient data, before framing his generalization. Though at that time many parts of the world were not much known ethnographically and he could not have much knowledge about them, he did not utilise fully, even if the data was available to him, such as Captain Cook's, least it may have gone against his views. Thus here as elsewhere, Morgan seems to have committed the fallacy of non-observation.

Morgan was also much inclined to generalise about the primitive world. In one of his theories about the primitive world, he made a remark that monarchy cannot appear prior to civilization. This generalisation also, we find, was on the basis of his own research in only the areas which he had come across. He had observed many primitive tribes, mostly Red Indians, organised on the democratic principle. But in making such a remark, it is indeed a pity that he ignored the African and Polynesian facts. However, excuse to this we can find for him, if we are aware of the fact of his being essentially an evolutionist and that too of unilinear school. As was customary with the evolutionists of this line to seek the same scheme of sequence of things in all the parts of the world, Morgan in doing so, was only following the tradition.

On the Sib-organization also, Morgan's contribution is noteworthy. He has expounded his theory of the origin of Sib-organization in the *Ancient Society*. Sib-System in Morgan's view arose as a result of a reformatory movement.

Morgan believed in a promiscuous stage which preceded civilization. This was the time when promiscuity in its full form prevailed, and there were no regulations for it. At such a stage, in Morgan's view, there were no forms of marriage nor of family. Because of promiscuity, inbreeding prevailed, which resulted in the deterioration of the stock. As men became conscious of this degeneration of the race because of close-inbreeding they tried to check it by adopting some measure. And they adopted this measure to check inbreeding by introducing Sib-system. Morgan in his *Ancient Society* writes : "Sibs arose because of a remarkable reformatory movement that retrenched intermarriage of blood relatives, gained a foothold through a biologically beneficial result thereby and spread its consequence over an enormous area.

Morgan seems to argue here in favour of his theory, very logically, though how far scientifically, still remains a question to decide. The following points are involved in his arguments in favour of the theory :

(i) That people had become cognizant of racial deterioration resulting from inbreeding, and wanted to reform it.
(ii) For this reason they introduced the Sib-system which proved beneficial in its effects.
(iii) Because of these favouring results, the sibs were further spread over enormous areas, i.e. all over the world.

All these arguments have been severally challenged by his critics.

First of all, they point out, how could men in such an early stage of social development, be able to devise social-institutions so high in kind. Besides this, Morgan's theory of Sibs has been subjected to two more points of criticism.

(i) its pretended distribution, and
(ii) alleged beneficial effects of the sib-system.

Scrutinising Morgan's theory of Sibs on these we find that firstly, sib is not universal as was pre-supposed by Morgan. There are many tribes even today who have no sib-organization, such as the Sakai and Semon who live an isolated life, lack the sib-organization. In Africa, Bushmen, Hottentotts and Pygmies (Negritoes) have no sib-system. We also notice that it is the family which is universal and found to exist all levels of civilization. Sibs are only a late product and develop probably when a tribe passes from hunting to a pastoral stage. There are many tribes who have no sib-system, already noted above, but there is not a single human group or tribe found in the present or even reported in the past, without a family. Thus Morgan's claim for the universality of sibs does not hold ground.

As to the second argument of inbreeding as Hoebel has rightly pointed out : "The fact is that inbreeding does not necessarily produce physical deterioration. It depends on the nature of inbreeding-stock. Inbreeding does no more than to intensify the traits, the stock possessed at the outset. Nevertheless, it is true that inbreeding intensifies the influence of dominant traits."

Morgan would have found it very difficult to maintain his position against such acute criticisms.

Morgan pushed his theory still further to advocate the priority of 'matrilineal sibs' over the patrilineal. In this connection he argues that matrilineal sib was earlier, since family did not exist; and since knowledge of paternity did not exist; property passed on from mother to daughter. It was only later, according to Morgan, that male-children also began to claim inheritance as a result of jealousy.

Thus patrilineal sibs developed only after the recognition of father's role, in Morgan's view. But it is to be remembered that even in societies in which biological fatherhood is not recognised, sociological fatherhood plays an important social role, such as in the case of the polyandrous Todas of southern India. Thus, ethnographic evidence stands against Morgan's theory. Moreover, even in matriarchal societies, male inheritance is found to exist in some or the other form, such as the inheritance of magic spells and formula by the sons, hence we find, the cases of parallel inheritance are also found.

In the light of such facts, to posit the priority of one type of organization over the other would be as illogical as the case *vice-versa*. The only tangible solution to this seems that there may have been a parallel development of both of these institutions.

Morgan is also associated with a number of other things, such as his theory of "primitive promiscuity" referred to above and development of different forms of marriage from it, and his scheme of institutional progress. In chalking out such a scheme, it will be well to remember that he was no 'better' than his other contemporary writers on the same subject. He applied the same unilinear scheme, equally to the development of marriage, kinship, government and property. Again, an understanding of the position of Morgan indicates that he was exclusively an unilinear evolutionist and furnishes us with the clue to understand all his theories in that context.

Suggesting the development of marriage, Morgan starts, like the rest, with agamy, a time when there was no marriage, and complete indifference or promiscuity prevailed. He then has a second stage, which he calls the Melayan, or Consanguine family. Here the group is promiscuous but with limitation that only members of the same generation can inter-marry. This type of marriage is admitted to be a "pure deduction" from the classificatory system of Polynesia, in which each relationship is coterminous with the whole of its generation. It is indeed curious to find that such a system, so far removed from the primitive, should have been given so early place in the history of development, under Morgan's theory. The next sort of group-marriage is deduced from the relationship terms of the four-class systems, in which people now marry their cross-cousins. This, in Morgan's view, further limited promiscuity. The further development of other forms of marriage, Morgan traces through polyundry, polygyny to monogamy. Morgan's scheme of the development of various forms of marriage, in a typological series, is something like this from Agamy or primitive promiscuity to Group Marriage to Non-Fraternal Polyandry to Fraternal Polyandry to Monogamy (Voluntary) to Polygyny to Monogamy (Forced).

In this way, he chalked out a series of forms in the gradual evolution of the present form of marriage, i.e., monogamy.

This stage of development of marriage-forms was, however, severally challenged by this contemporary writer, Westermarck, who had become much famous because of his great work *History of Human Marriage*. Westermarck, as against Morgan, strongly maintained that man had never been promiscuous, and that he has ever been living under monogamy. Westermarck will have none of the doctrine of primitive promiscuity, arguing that no tribes of man in normal state live thus, and that the custom and relationship terms which have been taken as proof of such promiscuity do not, in fact, prove it. The fault with Morgan's theory, thus, lies in reading "unwarranted meanings" involved in the Polynesian data. The fault lies in the "disease of language" itself. In Polynesian language the terms for 'uncle' and 'begetter' are the same, and since European language has no separate kinship term for begettor, nor is it enjoined with 'uncle', what Morgan inferred on the basis of the above data was that it was a survival of the promiscuous stage, in which there may have been such incestous relations.

This is, however, no valid an explanation, but rather a weak point in Morgan's theory. It is like seeing things as one likes, and not as they "are". The subjective element becomes so dominant in such observation that it almost neglects the other side, and often distorts the view.

Morgan has interpreted other social usages also much in the same way, in correspondence with his unilinear scheme of evolution. To the practice of "avunculate" – a right of authority of uncle (mother's brother) over his nephews, he attributes the cause of being "survivals" from promiscuity. In the same way for the incest-taboo, he seems to suggest that it is as a result to check the harmful consequences of close-intreeding.

From all this, it is clear that Morgan being an unilinear evolutionist sought to make out a universal scheme of development of things, and easily took note of those facts only which fitted well into his theory. It is this reason why he neglected all other sides. He didn't care to study other aspects of culture and society, or other social institutions, and confined himself only to his one or two spheres. His attitude of negligence towards 'tribal religion' reflects in the following remark that he once passed : "All primitive religions are grotesque and unintelligible."

Morgan was also, like other evolutionists, engaged in the "reconstruction of the past". He divided history into three parts – (i) Savagery, (ii) Barbarism, and (iii) Civilization.

Savagery, according to Morgan was the period before the invention of pottery; Barbarism – was the period before the advent of script, and Civilization, the time which is correlated with the introduction of script or writing.

Being an unilinear evolutionist, he suggested that all humanity had 'evolved' through the above well-marked stages, before it reached its present form.

Reviewing all the above theories of Morgan and his view, as discussed above, we find that despite some of the deficiencies or weak points involved in his theories, and his assuming too much or too little evidence, and despite his being in the line of the more uncompromising evolutionists, "his contribution is far greater than that of other students of the marital and filial regulations of the society', and he has supplied us with such a valuable system the importance of which is now accepted all the world over. Besides his discovery of the classificatory-system, he is the inventor of a method, whereby social structure can be studied as a complex of interacting functions. Since his time, W.H.R. Rivers has developed the genealogical method in the field-work and has made clear how invaluable an instrument it is for understanding the inter-relations of a society. Much work, since then, has been done by Tylor, Radcliffe Brown and by a later writer, De-Forde, who developed the kinship-system still further, much on the lines of the method formulated by the first discoverer.

The value of Morgan's contribution, thus, cannot be over-emphasised, while it remains unchallenged.

5

Theories of Totemism and its Distribution in India

ALL The Primitive tribes have some form of social and religious organizations. An organization in which the features of the two are closely blended together is that of 'totemism'. In the cultures of many primitive tribes; features of religion and social organization are combined in a peculiar way. Anthropologists call such tribes 'totemic', while designating as a 'totemic complex' the sum total of features, whether religious, ritualistic, social or artistic, which make up 'totemism'.

The term 'totem' in anthropology, literally means some 'symbol' or symbolic object. 'Totemism' thus means a belief in some totemic object – which may be an animal or a plant and a belief in deriving the descent from that totemic object. On no other subject, so much attention has been focused and so much written by the social anthropologists as on totemism. Durkheim has furnished us with a fully elaborate scheme of totemism from his observations in a detailed account of totemism in Australia. He regarded totemism as the archaic of all religious life and the earliest form of religion.

Totemism is one of the most widespread institutions of primitive society. It is found in North America in several wide-flung areas; as our knowledge of South-America increased, totemism there seems to be almost equally common; it is also found in Africa.

In Australia totemism is practically universal, and it is found, in function or at least in traces, in several of the island clusters of Melanesia.

In India totemism is almost scattered all over the country, and in some form or the other, both primitive as well as many of the modern Hindu communities show indications of a belief in some form of totemism. Goldenweiser, a supposed authority on the subject, called the totemism in India, in "a crude, or moribund form". In India many tribes and castes are found to claim mystic ties with some material object, animal or plant species. They certainly are the totemistic people though many of these have either forgotten their totem or do not attach much importance to such mystic connection. Thus almost all the castes following Hinduism show a strong feeling of veneration towards the cow; the killing of which is taken as the most repugnant action and is a strict taboo–made strong and fast both by religious as well as social factors, the violation of which is a serious religious and social offence which may lead even to the expulsion of the offender from the caste and society.

This is surely a feature of totemic organization a taboo imposed against the 'totemic' object.

The other feature in which many of even the modern communities can be said to show traces of totemism is the practice by them of the clan–exogamy. Clan-exogamy is said to be an important feature or rather an indispensable condition of totemism.

We shall be discussing in brief the distribution of totemism in India, referring to some of the main totemic tribes of India. In India, we find a large number of tribes are either organized on a totemic basis, or they hold animals and plants as sacred or observe taboos regarding eating or killing the animal or destroy the plant. Before referring to the distribution of totemism in India, let us examine here, some of the theories, put forward by different writers for the origin of totemism.

An institution so general in primitive society and in it alone, we find, is evidently tied to it by bonds far from casual. An understanding of totemism seems imperative in order to understand primitive life and thought.

In his Presidential address, before section H, *Anthropology of the British Association for the Advancement of Science*, A.C. Haddon referred to totemism in the following terms :

> Totemism, as Dr Frazer and I understand it in its fully developed condition, implies the division of a people into several kins (or, as they are usually termed, 'totem clans') each of which has one or sometimes more than one totem. The totem is usually a species of animal, sometimes a species of plant, occasionally a natural object or phenomenon, very

rarely a manufactured object. 'Totemism also involves the rules of exogamy, forbidding marriage between the kins. It is essentially connected with the matriarchal stage of culture (mother right), though it passes over into the patriarchal stage (father-right).

The totems are regarded as the kinsfolk and protectors of the kinsmen, who respect them and abstain from eating and killing them. There is thus a recognition of mutual rights and obligations between the members of the kin and their totem. The totem is the crest or symbol of the kin.

This is rather a comprehensive definition of totemism and includes almost all the specific features of a totemic organization.

Radcliffe Brown, another eminent writer in social anthropology in the modern times has also shed some light on the subject.

When used in a wider sense, he says, the term 'totem' is applied to wherever, "a society is divided into groups and there is a special relation between each group and one or more classes of objects, that are usually natural species of animals or plants, but may occasionally be artificial objects or parts of an animal. Used in a narrow sense, he further suggests, it is applied only when the groups in question are clans, i.e. exogamous groups of closely related kins by descent in one line. He regards clan totemism as only one variety of totemism in the wider sense of the term.

Theories of Origin of Totemism

Now, having given some of the current views about totemism by some of the main authors, let us now examine some of the theories of origin.

In speculating about totemism some authors were primarily concerned with its origin while others attempted to place totemism against the background of primitive mentality or to indicate its place in the evolution of religion. The name "totem" was first learned from the North American Indians by the Englishman. I. Long in 1791. I. J. McLennan was the first to understand the significance of totemism as a primitive social institution. Durkheim later carried on an intensive work on totemism basing his researches on the Australian totemism, which he considered to represent the most primeval form of religious life.

The Nickname Theory of Spencer and Andrew Lang

Totemism was conceived as a "system of naming" by Major Powell, a theory partially maintained also by Piler and Sorlo and by Herbert Spencer. In the form given to it by the latter author the theory became known as the "misrepresentation of nick-names" theory. Spencer assumed that animal names were once given to individuals, that these names were subsequently confused with the animals themselves owing to the vagueness of primitive languages, and ultimately such animals came to be worshipped as ancestors.

Andrew Lang, who, is remembered for his theories related to religion, in his work, *Secret of the Totem* (1905) partially subscribed to the naming theory with two important modifications. He held that, for one reason or another, the animal's names were first applied to the social groups, not to individuals, that later the origin of these names was forgotten, and speculate guesses were made by the primitives as to the provenance of the names. Thus the stage was set for a totemic origin. "No more than these three things – argued Lang – a group animal name of unknown origin; belief in a transcendental connection between all bearers, human and bestial, of the same name; and belief in the blood superstitions were needed to give rise to all the totemic creeds or practices including exogamy.

Frazer's Three Theories

Frazer, who launched totemism upon its busy career and years later continued the subject his massive four volumes' work on *Totemism and Exogamy* (1910) entertained at different times three different theories of totemic origin. The first became known as the "outward soul" or "bush soul" theory, the second as the "cooperative Magic" theory and the third as the "conceptional" theory.

The "outward soul" Theory

Initially, Frazer held that totemism developed out of the tucking away of human souls in animals, for preservation or safety. This enhanced the religious status of the animals. As it was not known, moreover, in which particular animal of a species the "bush-soul" had its abode, the custom in time led to the veneration of the entire species.

The "Cooperative magic" Theory :
(Intichiuma ceremonies).

Frazer's second hypothesis was suggested by the *intichiuma* ceremonies described by Spencer and Gillen (1899) in their work on the Central Australians. These ceremonies which have since been discussed so much, consist in somewhat dramatic rituals in which the natives dance and sing their magical rites for the multiplication of the totem animals. Each gens in the Central Australia has the exclusive right to perform the *intichiuma* for its own totem animal. From the resulting enhancement of the species, the gens itself does not, to be sure, derive benefit, for the totem is taboo to its members, but the other gens do benefit.

"In short", writes Frazer, "totemism among the Central Australian tribes appears, if we may judge from the *intichiuma* ceremonies, to be an organized system of magic intended to procure for savage man a plentiful supply of all the natural objects whereof he stands in need". Then, the wanting enthusiastic proceeded further. The author adds: "The thought naturally presents itself to us : 'Have we not in these ceremonies found the key to the original meaning and purpose of totemism among the Central Australian tribes, perhaps even of totemism in general."

The "Conceptional" Theory

Further, pondering over the Australian material, meanwhile amplified by Spencer and Gillin's second study (1904), led to the formulation of the third and final theory of Frazer, the "Conceptional" theory (1905). According to this theory, it appeared that these natives ascribed conception, the physiology of which was to obscure to them, to the impregnation of women by spirits or spirit carriers which they encountered, or thought they did, at the sacred totem spots, haunted by the spirits. "If we use what in particular may have suggested the theory of conception which appears to be the tap-root of totemism", says Frazer, "It seems probable that as (I have) already indicated, a preponderant influence is to be ascrbed to the sick fancies of pregnant women, and that so far, totemism may be described as a creation of the faminine rather than of the masculine mind. "With this contribution to the psychology of the sexes, Frazer's speculations about totemism came to an end.

These theories of Spencer, Lang and Frazer have been called the 'Nominalistic' theories of totemism which derived the origin of totemism from an association with the names in some form or other.

The "Sociological" Theories
Peter Schmidt's theory

Then there are the sociological' theories to totemism, which we shall now be discussing here.

Peter Schmidt, the then editor of the *Anthropos*, saw the origin of totemism, at least in Australia and certain parts of the South seas region, and in primitive trade.

He observed that in Mabuiag the two totems used in the magical fertilization ceremonies are also the principal, or perhaps, only articles employed in inter-tribal trade.

Reflection over this fact led to a theory which deduced totemism "seemingly so mysterious" from a "relatively prossaic and simple source." "Who does not recognize the familiar fact", writes the author in substance," that our peasants often abstain from using in their own households the food products they cultivate, but export them mostly to the neighbouring town?"

Local products intended for trade, are tabooed to the inhabitants of the district. The food interdict, an economic custom in origin, becomes in time a moral law, and after a while the original motive of the interdict is forgotten.

There followed a time of doubt and uncertainty, quotes the author, "conditions pregnant with metaphysical associations." In recognition of its importance in the life of the tribe, it is suggested, the animal or plant becomes the mythical source of the life of the tribe, its ancestor. And thus it became natural then that the group should assume or be called by the name of the animal or plant, so plentiful in its district.

After advancing a further argument in favour of the priority of plant-magic over animal-magic, Schmidt concludes that garden-culture was the cradle of the magical multiplication rites: "I believe that these things develop quite naturally out of plant cultivation followed by trade; starting from this base, the subsequent developments in the sphere of mythology explain equally naturally all the details of the fertilization rites and of the peculiar totemism of the northern Australians. This theory, extravagant though it might seem, does not stand alone, for it was anticipated by A.C. Haddon, who in 1902 advanced a very similar theory even though less elaborately argued.

There were besides these other theories, one such holding that totemism grew out of the worship of individual guardian spirits; and the other, of Graebner, being based on the diffusionist principles, identified totemism with localization and paternal descent, forming a culture area.

Let us, now turn to some other important theories of totemism, such as Durkheim, Wilhelm Wundt, and Sigmend Freud.

Durkheim's Sociological Theory of Totemism

Among all the theories of totemism suggested, Durkheim's sociological theory of totemism deserves special mention as it occupies the most important place.

Durkheim developed his theory of totemism in his *Elementary Forms of the Religious Life : Totemic System in Australia (1915).*

"Religion" Durkheim held, "is a complex of beliefs and activities referring to sacred things, and the characteristic fact in all religions is the division of beings, things and activities into sacred and profane."

If Australian totemism is a genuine religion, it must be the most primitive type of religion, for the social organization of the Australians is the most primitive known to us, based on the clan.

We note the following points in Durkheim's totemism.

The totemic symbol or emblem is the expression of the social solidarity of the clan mates. The symbol as the name of the clan is derived from the animal or plant which happens to be the most common in the locality where the clan congregates. Totemic rituals arise spontaneously as a direct expression of certain wishes regarding the food supply, and, whether imitative or representative, these rituals arouse pleasurable sensations in the participants by raising their social consciousness. These feelings of satisfaction are projected into the realm of physical nature, giving rise to the belief in the efficacy of the ritual. The unusual experiences accompanying the periodic ceremonial gatherings, when contrasted with the routine happenings of daily life, awaken in the mind of the totemite a sense of the sacred. Not being aware of the source of their exhaltation, the individuals of the clan identify the sacred with the totemic symbols by which they find themselves surrounded on these ritualistic occasions. The true constant of their beliefs, however, consists of a vague undifferentiated sense of an impersonal principle, prototype of "mana", but unlike "mana", the totemic principle, instead of becoming generalized, remains associated with the specific characteristics of the clans.

The totem represented in the symbols partakes of its nature and sacred character. The totemites having become identified with the totem the name of which they bear, are, as such also sacred. The entire physical universe, under such scheme, is classified in accordance with the phratries and clans, and the beings and objects thus classified with a certain totem share its sacred character.

Thus totemism, Durkheim suggests, should be regarded as a religion not of the clan but of the tribe, each clan being sympathetically aware of the beliefs and practices of the other clans which, moreover, strictly correspond to its own. Individual totemism is a derivative of clan totemism, and sex totemism partakes of the nature of both. The individual soul is an incarnation of the spiritual essence of a totemic ancestor. The soul of these mythical totemic personages live on as spirits, the more prominent among them developing into tribal gods.

Thus totemism is revealed as a genuine religion. It compares a division of beings, things and activities into sacred and profane; it engenders the belief in souls, spirits and gods; it has its cosmology; and its elaborate rituals embrace a form of sacrifice and ascetic practices. At the root of this religion lies the belief in a totemic principle, a belief which expresses the reaction of an individual psyche to its experience of the social control exercised by the clan. Indeed, the totemic principle, is the clan. Society : God. To Durkheim, the totem, animal or plant is the collective representation of the social mind.

Durkheim's theory of totemism is essentially religious. A social group such as a clan can only possess the solidarity and permanence, if it is the object of sentiments of attachment in the minds of its members. For such sentiments to be maintained in existence, they must be given occasional collective expression.

Durkheim compares the 'totem' of a clan with the flag of a nation. This comparison is valid in a very general sense according to Radcliffe Brown, for some forms of totemism, if not all. The function of the ritual towards the totem is, for Durkheim, to express and so to maintain in existence, the solidarity of the social group.

"Totemism for Durkheim, is not a system of magic, it is not zoolatry; it is not derived from "ancestor-worship" as some thought, nor a case of "nature-worship" as some others did, nor a contrivance to put the soul in safety."

It is also not to be explained as the consequence of the mere adaption of a name by a group. It is genuine religion, for Durkheim, "the most elementary form hitherto discovered, and is bound up with the most elementary form of social organization. For religion is not simply a social phenomenon, it is society seeking to realise itself. Society cannot exist apart from religion, and men are not men apart from society.

The term "totem", thus we see is the "emblem of the clan", that by which it recognises its unity itself. This accounts for the fact that the representation of the totem or *churinga, nurtunja, waninga* and elsewhere in the Australian tribes, is even more sacred than the sacred species. But alike the totemic species, the representation of the totem, all things associated in the categories with the totem, and the very members of the clan, themselves became sacred, though not in the same measure. They are all filled with supernatural force, physical and moral, with "wakan", 'orenda" and "mana" or whatever it may be called. This force is impersonal. It permeates all things. It is at the root of all religion and magic. Durkheim illustrates his totemism by referring to the Australian ceremonials and assemblies. The religious activity is confined to these ceremonies in Durkheim's view. Since they are centred around the totem, the totem arouses religious forces, which dominate and exalt the individuals and which are figured as an element or plant, or whatever the other object it may be that gives its name to the clan and serves as its emblem.

"The totem" then is nothing other than the clan under a material and emblematic form."

The soul is the totemic principle incarnated and individualised in each member of the clan.

According to the Durkheimian interpretation, thus, the reality is the society, the clan which really does inspire him. The function of the rites, is, in fact, to strengthen the bonds of the individual to the society.

In the case of primitive man, Durkheim contends that the religious sentiment would be inspired primarily not by society as a whole, but by the immediate grasp with which he is related, viz., the totemic clan.

Thus we find that according to Durkheim's analysis, the most fundamental belief implicit in totemism, is the belief in a mysterious and sacred force, or principle, which animates the totem, provides a physical sanction for violation of the totem taboo, and inculcates moral responsibilities.

The totem is to be considered, thus, only as a symbol. It symbolizes first the sacred totemic principle or god, and second, the clan itself, with which the totem is closely identified. Durkheim infers from this that the "totemic divinity" and the clans are really the same thing, and more generally, that "God" is only "a symbolic expression of the society".

Durkheim, as we have noted, finds the basis of earliest form of religion in the Australian totemism. As has been said about Sir Elliot Smith that his sojourn in Egypt had impressed him so much that he was fully convinced that Egypt and no other place, could have been the centre of all civilization which may have spread from there (Egypt) to other parts of the world; so the same is equally true about Durkheim, that his observation of totemism in Australia had impressed him so much that he regarded the Australian totemism as the earliest or most primeval form of all religious life. Thus, we find that "in casting about for the key to the mystery of religion, that is of its origin, Durkheim goes to the Australians because they are said to represent the primitive conditions of human communal life in his view" – remarks Lowie. Their concepts of sacredness are all wrapped in totemic ritualism, hence the essence of their totemism becomes the essence of archaic religion.

Thus we find Durkheim's theory of totemism also becomes his theory of the origin of religion. There can be no dispute that his totemistic theory is founded on sound logical corrollaries, yet they are not devoid of some of the grave errors, which points out that they probably left for their critics to attack at.

Criticism of Durkheim's Theory

The Sociological Theory of totemism suggested by Durkheim is subjected to much criticism by Goldenweiser and Lowie. Thus this criticism is based mainly on the ethnological, the sociological and the psychological grounds.

Goldenweiser's Criticism

From the ethnological point of view, Goldenweiser asks whence the non-totemic peoples have derived their religion. Totemism, as we know from the ethnographical evidence, is not universal.

On Ethnological Evidence

The ethnological evidence at our hand shows that there are many primitive and some of the simplest tribes in both the Old and the New World, which lack sibs and totems. No such institution is found among the Andaman Islanders, who are considered to be one of the most primitive peoples in the world, yet they have religion. So also the same can be said about the Chukchi of Siberia, who too have no totemic organization. In short, there are many non-totemic peoples and amongst them precisely there are those of the simplest culture, but they all have some sort of religion. Thus absence of sib or clan organization and totemism does not necessarily mean the absence of religion also. The clan is not the oldest type of social unit, as we know, having been preceded by the society. Australian society is, in fact, not the simplest known, but it is manifestly more complex than that of Fuegians, the Basin and Californian Indians, the Eskimo, or the Andamanese.

To learn about the origins of religion from them, and through Australian totemism, is, thus, accordingly hopeless, and "such an attempt is a relapse into unilinear evolutionism" in the words of Lowie. Durkheim, like Frazer, has been deceived by the rash assumption that the primeval culture of humanity is represented in Australia.

On Sociological Grounds

From the sociological angle, Goldenweiser objects that while ostensibly Durkheim defies the society, his conception of it in the role of God is a singularly narrow one, since he practically identifies society with crowd at another place – (his interpretation of the crowd phenomena).

He also ascribes Australian religious activities to be restricted to assemblies and the tribal God, who is sacred, is only a product of the tribal sentiment, which he calls "Crowd–phenomena." Hence, here it is the 'crowd phenomena' which becomes sacred, and the individual by merging himself into this loses his identity and is profane. Thus this view of Durkheim is also vitiated by the same defects, since this has also a reference to the clan as the earliest form of organization.

On Psychological Grounds

On psychological ground also Durkheim's totemistic theory has been disputed.

Durkheim shows a tendency of aversion to psychology, yet he relapses into it, taking its recourse to build up his theory of totemism and to explain the behaviour of the individual members of the clan. he seems to smuggle into psychology for his evidence for explaining the "crowd phenomena." His conception of "crowd-phenomena" is nothing but a product of his 'pure psychologising."

He reduced, moreover, the individual to mere automatan, and this again, on purely psychological grounds. He also lapses into psychology while talking about the uniformity of individuals and their behaviour to be stereotyped. Further, as Goldenweiser suggests, if a crowd situation precipitates religious behaviour and sentiment, why does he not hold this for all crowds? What distinguishes the secular from the ceremonial American Indian dance? Why does the Australian coroborce remain a form of entertainment, distinct from initiation and totemic rituals? Evidently there is a determinant over and above the mere factor of assemblage. Durkheim has not ventured to answer all these points. He rather seems to have misapplied the psychological data. It is in such cases that Durkheim's theory of totemism succumbs to the criticisms.

Further more, to add to these criticisms suggested, we find, there are some other weak points in Durkheim's sociological theory of totemism.

In Durkheim's sense, totemism certainly qualifies as a religion, a tribal, not a clan religion, for it belongs to the domain of the sacred, not profane, in the primitive life.

But it must never be forgotten, that the religious attitude toward the totem is scarcely ever pronounced; also that totemism, in "no" instance constitutes the whole or even the centre of the religious aspect of a tribal culture.

"Animism, ancestor or nature-worship, fetichism, idolatory, or even animal or plant worship, suggests, Goldenweiser, "may reach and all be present in a totemic tribe, side by side with totemism". Again any of these features may become assimilated with a totemic complex in a particular place, so as to form an integral part of it, or they may not.

Thus in summarising the case we can say that though Durkheim's totemistic theory errors at some place, and is largely defective at many other, it cannot be denied at the least the partial validity. It contains some ingredient element of truth in so far as it emphasizes the superiority of society over individuals, as well as it indicates one essential feature of totemism – its relation with the clan-system. So far it would continue to have its validity.

Wundt's Theory

Apart from the theories discussed above, there are two more important ones, those of Wundt and Freud which seek to explain the origin of totemism.

To Wundt, totemism appears of interest from two angles. He places the origin of the institution in the period when the belief in a breadth or shadow soul became differentiated from the earlier belief in a body soul. The first totem animals, therefore, were the soul animals, hawk crow and lizard in Australia, eagle, falcon and snake in America–in which human souls were deposited. As a culture historian, on the other hand, Wundt, conceives of totemism as providing the socio-psychological and ideological background of nothing less than a "totemic era", one of the four or five culture eras into which the history of mankind can be divided. With the totemic era, Wundt identifies clan organization, exogamy, chieftainship, animal and plant culture, native myths, zoomorphic and phytomorphic cults and a number of other cultural features.

Freud's Theory of Totemism

Then there is, Freud's theory of totemism, strange as are his other theories with pseudo-psychological tinge, expounded in his book *Totem and Taboo.* The theory of Freud, runs, in brief, as follows:

In very early times, before there was any definite social organization or religion, man lived in so-called cyclopean families in which all the sex rights were monopolized by the dominant old man, while the younger men, his sons, had to submit to the restrictions imposed by him or be killed or expelled from the group. The great dominant male, the father was revered by the others for his powers and wisdom, but he was also hated on account of his monopolistic prerogatives. One day a great tragedy was enacted in such a primitive community. The brothers banded together – encouraged perhaps by the invention of a new weapon – and dared to do openly together what each one had long secretly desired.

They murdered the father (the dominant old man), and consumed his body in the assurance of thus acquiring his prowess. The practical act having been committed the sons, tortured by remorse, reverted to a positive attitude toward the father. Obsessed by a belated desire to be obedient to him, they decided to continue the taboo, the oppressive character of which had led to the murder, and to abstain from sex contact with the women of the group. The consciousness of common guilt became the root of the new social bond. Thus arose the clan, protected and reinforced by the taboo on killing a clanmate, in order that the fate of the father might not befall any of the brothers. The totem of the clan is therefore but a transfigured image of the father, and the totemic sacrifice, an occasion for both joy and sorrow, but a dramatization of the remote tragedy in which the jubiliant brothers murdered their despot father; conscience-stricken, reimposed upon themselves the oppressive taboo in the name of which the murder had been committed.

Freud goes still further. In the control setting of Greek tragedies he discovers another cultural symbolization of the gruesome event of earliest antiquity. The hero's past is to suffer, suggests Freud, for he is but the dramatized memory of the murdered father, whereas the responsive chorus stands for the patricidal brothers. In this new setting, however, their part in the original tragedy is disguised under the cloak of a positive attitude toward the hero, a psychological subterfuge with which, in the domain of the individual psyche, psychoanalytic has made us familiar.

The four institutions: Thus under Freud's scheme, four great institutions of mankind are ultimately reducible to one basic and pregnant event, a common psycho-sociological source.

(i) Common guilt lay at the root of the new social system, the clan in primitive society.

(ii) The consciousness of guilt expressed itself in a regard for the totem father in the earliest Religion.

(iii) In expiation of the crime came the self-imposed rule of exogamy, primal sex taboo and the earliest embodiment of Morality.

(iv) In the dominant of Art, finally, Greek tragedy re-enacted the ancient deed in an expiatory disguise.

Thus Freud's theory gives a strange explanation of the origin of totemism.

A Review of the Totemistic Theories

"Details apart, a review of these theories leaves one with the impression that when we say "totemism" we have said all there is to be said about the history of human civilization. Give a speculator a thread, and he will enmesh the world", remarks Goldenweiser reviewing all these psycho-sociological theories.

The totemic origin theories which seek the first origin of totemism in some one of its features – name, descent zoolatry trade, magic co-operation, ideas of conception – all suffer from dogmatic one-sidedness. With reference to a particular or another of these theories may prove correct, but no ground is forthcoming why almost any of the others might not apply at some other place. It must be granted, however, that the theories stressing the totemic clan name come nearer to the essence of the problem than do the others. Even though this feature of the nominalistic view is not universal in totemic complexes, it is exceedingly common and must have provided in many, if not most instances, the link between the mystical and the social elements in totemism. Through the name, the locus and limits of each particular totemic connection – a particular clan with a particular totem – must have been established in numerous cases.

The theories stressing the role of totemism in religious evolution are in the wrong in so far as they overemphasize the religious aspect of totemism and assume its universality.This stricture applies particularly to Ievon's *Introduction to the History of Civilization.* In Durkheim's view as we have said above, totemism certainly qualifies as a religion, a tribal not a clan religion, for it belongs to the domain of the sacred, not the profane, in primitive life. But it must never be forgotten that the intensity of the religious attitude toward the totem is scarcely even pronounced; also that totemism in no instance constitutes the whole or even part of its religious aspect.

Animism, ancestor or nature worship, fetichism, idolatory or even animal or plant worship – may reach to any objective and all be present in a totemic tribe, side by side with totemism. Again, any of these features may become assimilated with a totemic complex in a particular place, so as to form an integral part of it, or they may not.

Writers like Wundt, and finally, Lawrence Gomme in his *Folklore as a Historical Science* who speak of a "totemic era" and the like, err in two important respects. On the one hand; they once more assume the universality of totemism of which, to say, the least, there is no evidence. On the other hand, they identify with totemism, genetically as a historic co-existence a variety of cultural features and tendencies, which have nothing whatever to do with totemism either psychologically or culturally or historically, even though they will occur in totemic tribes and cultures.

By contrast with the older theories of totemism who were, as a rule, concerned with the similarity and unity of totemic phenomena, Goldenweiser suggests in *Totemism: An Analytic Study* (1910), the "diversity of totemic complexes" and "the psychological and historical heterogeneity of the features entering into these complexes", which seems more easily admissible than any other.

Basic Characteristics of Totemism

Having now discussed various theories of the totemic origin, let us examine in brief the basic characteristics of totemism which characterize almost all totemic organizations.

Exogamy and the taboo on the totem (the totemic object) are considered the two universal characteristics of all the totemic organizations.

Exogamy

Exogamy is said to be the first and foremost characteristic of all totemic organizations – whether primitive or modern. This exogamy, we note, is generally the clan-exogamy. An examination of a sufficient number of totemic complexes will show that exogamy, in one form or another, is almost always present.

Every clan has its totem and all the members of the clan are supposed to derive descent from the totem (totemic ancestor). Thus marriage between them would be ancestuous. Therefore, all totemic organizations prescribe exogamy and do not allow the marriage between the clan-members. This leads, thus we see, to the clan-exogamy which is strictly followed. In India, among the

Hindu castes, also we find this practice of clan-exogamy widely prevalent. The restriction on marriage between the members of the same '*gotra*' ('got') or clan so common, among the Brahmin and Kshatriya castes is only an illustration of the clan-exogamy.

Totemic Taboo

Second specific feature of totemism is the imposition of a taboo against killing or eating (or offending in any way) the totem. A relation between humans and the rest of nature, especially animals and plants is involved here. It may take the form of a "mystic affinity" or a belief in descent, or a taboo on the totem, or a mere eponymous function of the latter , without any associated beliefs or practices with reference to it. The veneration of cow and a strict taboo against its killing can be regarded as an illustration of this view.

Apart from these two basic theories of totemism there is a third feature of totemic organizations by which a tribal group may be divided into sub-groups or "phraeties" and "moieties ".

Distribution of Totemism in India

Let us now examine in brief the distribution of totemism in India. Goldenweiser thought totemism in India, prevalent as it is in numerous tribes, to be in "a crude, or perhaps, moribund form". But this seems rather hasty generalization.

In India many tribes and castes are found to claim mystic ties with some material object, animal or plant species.

These can certainly be taken to be the totemistic people, though they may not show the same degree of exactitude as do some other more primitive ones. Most totemistic tribes are either in the collectional stage or have learnt to supplement their gleanings from the forests and their humble gain from the chase, by crude farming such as by burning forests and sowing on the ashes. It is not surprising therefore that to find that animals and plants figure prominently in the totemic structure of primitive tribes and castes everywhere. Many totems are parts of animals, the liver, the heart, the entrails, or the juice of a flower or fruit and its kernel. Such partition of the totem animal or plant may have been necessitated by multiplication of original groups, as the same totemic group has split up into more than one totemic clan to meet the growing needs of social life. In Chota Nagpur, for example, when a totemic clan becomes numerically very large, it splits into sub-totems and the latter content themselves by adopting as their totem, parts of animal or plant which designated the larger division out of which they have regrouped themselves. Another fact can be noticed, usually neighbouring tribes living in the same geographical area possess similar totems though they do not recognize kinship obligation among them.

The Ethnographic Survey of India under the direction of Sir Herbert Risley collected relevant data on totemism and since then monographic studies of tribes have added to our knowledge of distribution of the institution. The Santhals, who form a considerable number of the tribal population of India, are largely totemistic. The Santhals have more than hundred clans, all named after plants, animals and materials objects. The Hos have more than 50 such clans, many being common with the Santhal. The Mundas are divided into more than 64 exogamous clans. Although inter-tribal relations are not much recognized, the various tribes of the Munda racial stock own similar totems, and most of these have some use to the tribes, either as edible fruits, roots, plants, and animals, or are injurious or harmful birds or animals, all found in the areas they inhabit.

The Bhils are divided into 24 clans, some of which are named after animals or plants. As they have been Hinduized and their origin and affiliation are still difficult to ascertain, the clan names may not give any clue to their social structure. Many tribes in Orissa, the Kurmi, the Kumar, the Bhumia, who have advanced in culture in recent years, are named after serpents, pumpkin, jackal and other totems. The Katkaris of Bombay, the Gond tribes of Madhya Pradesh and some of the tribes living in the Central India Agency (now largely forming Madhya Bharat and Vindhya Pradesh regions) also have clan names after the fauna and flora of their habitat. The Dhelki Kharias, a major section of Kharias of Chhota Nagpur plateau, are divided into 8 totemic clans. The Murias of Bastar are also largely totemistics, having the various animals as their totems.

The Murias in Bastar are divided into four totemic clans, named the Naitam, Marami, Sodi and Pojam. Each has its own totem in an animal, such as the tiger is the totem of Sodi (the word 'Sodi' itself meaning, a tiger in the tribal language), and that of Marami is a goat. Killing or eating of the totemic animal is a strict taboo to them.

Some Indian tribes are divided into 3, 4 or more phratries and some of the clans in a phratry may have an animal and plant name. Some of the tribes are also, organized into totemic organizations on the territorial basis.

In India – we find, even persons belonging to higher castes offer sacrifices and prayers to objects of nature as well as animal or vegetable species, rivers and rivulets are generally sacred and a regular cult is found about them. The 'tulsi', the 'bel', the 'box' are objects of worship, but these are not totems of social groups. In most parts of Eastern Bengal, the tiger has a cult and it is ceremonially worshipped on certain occasions, the monkeys and snakes are sacred to the Hindus; they would not kill or destroy either. The cat is protected by taboo and tradition. The killing of a cat is a taboo and the man who has done the offence, has to expiate his remissness. The cow is said to represent all the deities known to the Hindus. She is considered to be the abode of all 'Rishis'. Thus we find that a large number of animals and plants are venerated by the Hindus, the offence to which is tabooed and is highly punishable.

Stories of clan origin are many and can be cited in their hundreds. Some of the stories connected with the origin of totem clans among Ho, Munda and the Santhal explain how the totemic relation has emerged out of dire necessity at a time, when human help could not be requisitioned or was of little avail. Analysis of such evidence, from the totemic organizations of India, leads us to conclude that the spirit of totemism is to be sought not in a religious attitude toward totemic objects or emblem, not in a gradual process of postulating in totems the higher powers or spirits who influence the destiny of the savage, nor in the social or economic necessity of preserving species of edible products of the vegetable and animal kingdoms, but in a simple adjustment of social order which could bring about a sympathetic relation between man and his environment. Such a relation subserves the needs of human adaptation to the habitat, "So far as Indian totemism is concerned" says Majumdar, "an accidental connection between a group of animal or vegetable species seems to have been the rule, as will be evident from a number of examples found in India".

This is why Risley, who recorded the evidence of totemism and totemic survivals, could not vouchsafe for the religious aspect of totemism in India, and assumed that religious side of totemism was in "disuse", but the social side, i.e., exogamy, was invariably associated with totemism. The theories, we notice, centre around an arbitrary aspect of totemism which has been arrived at by first shuffling the so-called totemic state, divorced from their respective cultural background and then searching for their common denomination.

The totemless Hindus, and many aboriginal groups who are not totemistic are exogamous, while members of the same totemic clan may and often do marry among themselves. The various hypotheses we know of exogamy do not warrant a supposition that totemism and exogamy are casually connected. Frazer held that totemism and exogamy are distinct in origin and nature, though these have crossed and blended in many tribes.

Thus we notice that totemism in India is widely distributed, being scattered in various parts among the tribal as well as Hindu population, though in different form.

In conclusion we can say, that totemism is a common, though not a universal organization, often blended in strange way with the social and religious aspects of primitive society. Yet it is so important that an insight into its right understanding enables us to understand primitive social organization as such.

6

Anthropology of Magic, Science and Religion

EVERYWHERE In The world, there seems to be a longing or desire in man to know the mystery of the universal or to control the course of events if he could. He always seeks some casual relation behind the events of his life. But where he fails to discover and such necessity he surrenders to some unseen force, which he thinks, controls his destiny. It is in such condition that belief in religion arises.

But at the same time man also tries first to control the Universe, or the course of events. And here the magic makes its pace in the man's life. It gives him confidence and faith in his craving.

Magic and religion are thus closely, related, or rather they are the two aspects of the same thing. This relation becomes still closer in case of primitive people.

The primitive man was thought to consider himself no less powerful than gods or spirits. In reality the belief meant, that primitive man had some conception of superior or other powers and that he thought himself powerful to control those powers by means of his own skill.

Magic and medicine is supposed to be a stage earlier to religion. Under religion, man does not think of controlling these powers, but submits himself to these powers. He feels that he is unable to face these powers, because the power is "indefinite, invisible and invincible."

Primitive man finding himself unable to control the spirits and powers was compelled to surrender to them or please them by offering gifts, sacrifices, prayers etc. Man who had started with magic spells, now came to prayers, worship and propitiations. And hence, the magician converted himself to a priest. "A slight change in the methodology, a twist in the singing of the spells a bit more controlled the activities brought in the era of prayers and propitiations.

"Religion established to itself", according to this suggestion by these writers, "as soon as man realised his own weakness in comparison to alien powers, and submitted himself to them and started making efforts to please them."

This approach to explain magic and religion, attempts to show that magic is earlier and that religion establishes itself later, when man realises its necessity. Thus according to this approach to magic and religion, there should be people advanced in culture, who may have all religion and no magic and also that the most primieval societies may be having magic as the only controlling force. But recent researches have been enough to prove that both primitive as well as modern communities have magic and religion both.

"There are several things, which man comes across in his life and which he cannot adequately understand and explain. Many happenings and incidents of everyday life cannot be explained in terms of cause and effect. There are several factors, which are beyond the control of man, but which still continue to influence his life vitally. Man has tried to work his relationship with these forces through the medium of supernaturalism. "Through magic and religion, he makes an effort to control the unseen power ,of the mysterious unknown. Religion is founded upon a belief in the supernatural. It is almost a universal aspect of man's culture" as S.C. Dubey tells us.

Now tracing the history, we find that the emphasis on the religions and magical – or ritualistic aspect has been not very old. The early records of the travellers, explorers and investigators had given a fascinating picture of the religious life which were based solely on hearsay and hasty generalizations and never on scientific evidences.

Spectacular ceremonies, queer rites and ward beliefs and practices were explained as the results of intellectual speculation or of the specifically "primitive" condition of "pre-logical" mentality. But little attempt was made to relate these beliefs and practice to every day life, to individual hopes and fears, or to the collective pursuits and organization of human communities.

"Religion and magic" as Ralph Piddington tells us, "can only be understood in terms of what they do, the needs which they satisfy, and the influence which they have on human behaviour."

Frazer's Treatment of Magic and Religion

The emphasis on magic and religion and the relationship between the two was the outcome of Frazer's writings. Sir James George Frazer had devoted completely 100 volumes of his *Golden Baugh* – a treatise on the primitive religion to the treatment of magic and religion.

It was Sir James George Frazer who first introduced the pragmatic element into the study of primitive religion by attributing its growth to an active desire for effective control of the phenomena of nature, rather than to passive impression derived from the contemplation of them. The sources of primitive religion he finds in the failure of magic to effect the desired results. "Magic", he believes to be "a mistaken application of principles of association" which properly employed, lead to science.

"Wherever sympathetic magic occurs in its pure unadulterated form, it assumes that in nature one ever follows another necessarily and invariably without the intervention of any spiritual or personal agency," Frazer writes in *The Golden Baugh*.

Magic and Science

Comparing the magic with science, he further states : "Its (magic's) fundamental conception is identical with that of modern science; underlying the whole system is a faith, implicit, but real and firm, in the order and uniformity of nature". The magician does not doubt that the same causes will always produce the same effects, that the permanence of the proper ceremony, accompanied by the appropriate spell, will inevitably be attended by the desired result unless indeed his incantations should chance to be thwarted and foiled by the more potent charms of another sources. He supplicates no higher powers, he sues the favour of no fickle and wayweird being; he abases himself before no lawful deity. Yet his power, great as he believes it to be, is by no means arbitrary and unlimit. He can wield it only so long as he strictly conforms to the rules of his art, or to what may be called the laws of nature as conceived by him."

Thus there is much conformity and similarity between magic and science, in Frazer's view, as far as the matter of basic principle is concerned. Both magic and science involve a belief – in the necessary causality in all events – i.e. given certain (feasible) conditions, certain causes will produce certain efforts.

Thus the analogy between the magical and the scientific conceptions of the world is close. In both of them the succession of events is perfectly regular and certain, being determined by immutable laws, the operation of which can be foreseen and calculated precisely; the elements of caprice, of chance and of accident are banished from the course of nature. Both of them open up a seemingly boundless vista of possibilities of him – who knows the causes of things and can touch the secret springs that set in motion the vast and intricate mechanisms of the world. "Hence the strong attraction which magic and science, alike have exercised on the human mind; hence the powerful stimulus that both have given to the pursuit of knowledge. "They lure the weary inquirer, the foot sore seeker" – writes Frazer, "on through the wilderness of disappointment in the present by their endless promises of the future; they take him upto the top of mountains and show him beyond the dark clouds and the rolling mists at his feet, a vision of the celestial city, far off, it may be, but radiant with unearthly splendour, bathed in the "light of dreams".

Magic is, thus, very closely related to science as both follow the same general principle and inviolable laws.

But being even so closely related to science, magic differs from science in many important aspects. "The fatal blow of magic" – suggests Frazer in this connection, "lies not in its general assumption of a succession of events determined by law, but in its total misconception of the nature of the particular laws which govern that succession".

Illustrating this, Frazer tells us that if we analyze the various cases of sympathetic magic which have passed in review in the preceding pages, and which may be taken as fair samples of the bulk, we shall find them to be all mistaken applications of one or the other two great fundamental laws of thought, namely, "the association of ideas by similarity" and "the association of ideas by continuity in space or time". Here Frazer also shows the difference between two forms of magic the 'imitative' or 'mimetic' – and 'sympathetic magic'. Sir James Frazer also drew a distinction between two varieties of what he called 'sympathetic magic', namely, "homeopathic" and "contagious" magic. Sympathetic magic is founded on Frazer's theory, on a "mistaken application of the principles of association, which may take two forms, based respectively upon similarity and contiguity. Thus there are two widespread types of sorcery, which exemplify the two kinds of magic. We can illustrate these two varieties of magic by means of examples.

In the one, an effigy of the victim is made in wax or some other substance, and is burned, pierced or otherwise injured in the belief that this will produce a similar effect on the victim. This is the practice of 'homeopathic' magic. In the other type, i.e., contagious magic, something which has been in close contact with the victim – an item of clothing, nail pairings, hair-clippings etc. – becomes an object of destructive magic.

In both cases, we find the emotional basis is similar, and hatred is expressed by destructive action against some material object which represents symbolically the hated person.

As Piddington remarks in this connection "The bodily expression involved in magic are thus not unlike such actions as the clenching of the fists in anger; or the action of the lips, as though expelling some unpleasant substance from the mouth in expressions of disgust. They are culturally standardized ways of expressing certain emotions for which they provide at least a "partial satisfaction".

Reverting to the problem of relationship between magic and religion, we find, following Frazer that the "principle of association in magic and science are excellent in themselves" "Legitimately applied they yield science; illegitimately applied, they yield magic, the bastard sister of science."

It is, therefore, a truism, almost a tautology, suggests Frazer, to say that all magic is necessarily false and barren; for were it ever to become true and fruitful, it would no longer be magic but science.

From the earliest times man has been engaged in a search for general rules whereby to turn the order of natural phenomena to his own advantage, and in the long search he has scraped together a great hoard of such maxims, some of them apparently real and some of them mere dross". "The true or golden rules constitute the body of applies science, which we call the arts; the false are magic". "Magic assumes occult causes, while science is interested in matter of fact causes".

This is, then, Frazer's interpretation of magic and religion, while he views both as closely related and based on the same general principle and basic assumption in inviolable law of universe, the distinction between them arises, as to the results they produce.

Science is the end-achieved or the total success; magic is a failure in reaching a desired end.

Magic and Religion

Magic is also closely related to religion. If magic is the next kin to science, let us see now, how it stands related to religion. But the view we take of that relation will necessarily be coloured by the idea formed of the nature of religion itself, hence it becomes necessary to define the conception of religion before proceeding to discuss its relation to magic.

What is Religion?

There is probably no subject in the world about which opinions differ so much as the nature of religion, and "to frame a definition of it which would satisfy every one must obviously be impossible as Frazer tells us. However, we shall examine here some of the important definitions of religion, given by various writers.

Tylor's Definition

Tylor has given a brief but precise and what he thinks a "minimum" definition of religion – as he defines it, as – "a belief in Spiritual Beings" – he correlates this definition of religion with that of Animism – his theory of religion. But this definition, as we know, does not take a comprehensive view of religion. Even having been granted that most of the primitive religions foster a belief in same form or rather in the Spiritual Beings, we find that there are also exceptions to this, such as that of Buddhism, which do not believe in the Spiritual Beings. Thus, this interpretation of religion fails to give an adequate explanation of religion hence not valid.

Max Muller

The German scholar, Max Muller defined religion, as "a longing or desire to know the unknown, unknowable and un-understandable" i.e., the infinite". But again, we find this applies more to the Aryan than any other form of religion.

Durkheim

Durkheim, the French scholar holds that religion cannot be defined by any definitions, but can be only understood with regard to its subject-matter. The work of Emile-Durkheim, the French sociologist, for the first time, shifted the emphasis in the study of primitive religion from the past to the present. He criticizes in detail the earlier theories of religion, the main point of his argument being that all regard religion as a survival of some elementary intellectual blunder, some primordial process of muddled thinking. Any such theory, he holds fails to explain why religion, founded upon a great illusion, should have survived so long and should play the part which it does in human communities. If, on the other hand, we regard religion as corresponding to some reality, as meeting some actual human requirement, this problem does not arise. The reality upon which religion is founded, is, for Durkheim, essentially social, and is based upon the solidarity and spiritual communion, which the individual feels with the fellow-members of his social group, and he proceeds to elaborate this theory in relation to Australian totemism.

According to Durkheim's view, religion consists of two things, beliefs and rituals.

Beliefs are static, rituals are dynamic 'Mere beliefs cannot constitute religion; it is the rites which bring conformity with nature. Beliefs may remain same as they are static, but rites change since they are dynamic. Mistakes of magic are set right by religion.

The main defect of Durkheim's view is that he regards social solidarity which is no where adequately defined, as an end in itself, and does not attempt to relate it to other aspects of native life, nor to individual urges, considered apart from "collective representations", superimposed upon the individual by society. Religion has an effect in expressing and maintaining social cohesion of a non-religious character. Concretely, for example, Australian totemic increase ceremonies do undoubtedly serve the function which Durkheim attributed to them, namely that of increasing the sense of the individual's participation in the life of his social group. But they do far more than this; in the first place, they possess a marked economic function; they imply organized co-operation in productive activities, and they are very definitely related to the practical pursuits of a hunting and collecting people; their control by the old men emphasizes the political organization of the community and their associated mythology is closely related to family life, through the totemic theory of reproduction.

The social solidarity, which they express, can therefore, only be understood by considering it in concrete terms; that is, in relation to the extraneous institutional activities in which they are so closely related.

Frazer's View of Religion

The last, but not the least, to consider is the view of Frazer with regard to religion, and it has a great bearing upon the present discussion as it would be clear, that it was Frazer who emphasized the close relaltionship between magic and religion. "By religion," Frazer understands, "a propitiation or conciliation of powers superior to man which are believed to direct and control the course of nature and of human life."

Frazer's View of Magic and Religion

In this sense, it will readily be perceived, as Frazer himself tells us, that religion is opposed in principle both to magic and science. For all conciliation implies that the being conciliated is a conscious or personal agent, that his conduct is in some way uncertain, and that he can be prevailed upon to vary it in the desired direction by a judicious appeal to his interests, appetites, or his emotions. In so far as religion assumes the world to be directed by conscious agents, who may be turned from their purpose by prayers, "it stands in fundamental antagonism to magic as well as to science", both of which take for granted that the course of nature is determined, not by the passions or caprice of personal beings, but by the operation of 'immutable laws' acting mechanically."

In magic, we are told, indeed, the assumption is only implicit, but in science it is explicit. It is true that magic often deals with spirit which are personal agents of the kind assumed by religion but whenever it does so in its proper form, it treats them exactly in the same fashion as "it treats inanimate agents, that is, it constrains or coerces instead of 'conciliating' or propitiating them as religion would do."

Yet this antagonism, familiar as it is to us, seems to have made its appearance comparatively late in the history of religion. "At an earlier stage", Frazer tells us in his *Golden Boughl* "the functions of the priest and sorcerer were often combined or, to speak more correctly, were not yet differentiated from each other."

To serve this purpose, we are told by an author 'man' wooed the good-will of gods or spirits by prayer and sacrifice, while at the same time he had recourse to ceremonies and forms of words which he hoped would of themselves bring about the desired result without the help of god or devil. In short, "he performed religious and magical rites simultaneously; he uttered prayers and incantations almost in the same breath, knowing or reckoning little of the theoretical inconsistency of his behaviour, so long as 'by hook or by crook' he contrived to get what he wanted." Instances of this fusion or confusion of magic with religion have already met us in the practices of Melanesians and of some East Indian islanders. The same confusion of magic and religion has survived among peoples; Frazer maintains, that have risen to higher levels of culture. It was ripe in ancient India, and ancient Egypt, it is by no means absent among the European peasantry at the present day. With regard to ancient India, we are told, as Frazer reminds us, that "the sacrificial ritual at the earlier period of which we have detailed information is pervaded with practices that breathe the spirit of most 'primitive magic'. Again the same writer observes that "the ritual of the very sacrifice for which the metrical prayers were composed is described in the other Vedic texts as reiterated from beginning to end with magical practices which were to be carried out by the sacrificial priests. In particular he tells us that the rites celebrated on certain occasions, such as marriage, initiation, and the appointment of a king, "are complete models of magic of every kind and every case, the forms of magic employed bear the star of the highest antiquity. "Ancient magic was thus, the foundation of religion."

Magic seeks directly to influence the natural sequence of cause and effect, and shares with science the fundamental belief that this sequence is absolute and invariable. But religion is restricted to a different assumption, namely, the belief in the existence of "powers superior to man which are believed to direct and control the course of nature and of human life." This stage of belief, which is a step beyond that of faith in magic is reached when man realizes the futility of his magical practices, and instead offers supplications to powers higher than to himself, who can, he believes, alter the normal sequence of cause and effect at his behest. This theory goes far beyond than any other in stressing the "past played by human needs in the genesis of religion" as well as philosophical speculation. Such speculations is held to be carried out under the st.mulus of man's desire to control life and nature in accordance with his own wishes, "a desire whose first manifestation is found in magic." But like the other theories, that of Frazer is "orientated from a specific point of view," based upon a desire to discover the origin of religion in the history of mankind, rather than to understanding the reality of existing religions, and the part which they play in living human cultures.

General Review of Magic and Religion

We find, that failures of magic are corrected by further magic and thus a vicious circle develops in this way, which has prejudiced the primitive man from the earliest times. In course of time, magic must be reinforced by supplicatory rites, for the essence of magic is coercion and when it fails, approach to the higher powers can only be effected through prayers and prescriptions which define the role of Gods and deities, or superior powers, in life and in the prosperity of the people. "When spell is transformed into prayer, magic yields to religion. Much of magic is at par with religion; both are based on a similar intellectual attitude, as both want to unravel the mystery of the world." While magic explains the ways in which things happen in terms of hidden force, religion does it in terms of deities, spirits and power. The magician's art and religious ritual are both meant to create an atmosphere of suggestibility and the technique employed by both is similar. The performanc of both is governed by traditional order and form, conformity to which is essential for success. In the Hindu temple, for example, an atmosphere of suggestibility is created by the character of religious architecture, dim and diffuse lighting, burning of incense, the queer dress of the priest and his peculiar habits which are known to the public and also by the use of an ancient or classical language, mysterious formula and sing song monologue etc. "The difference between magic and religion lies therefore," to quote Majumdar, in the manner in which the mystery of the world is viewed. Magic represents an exaggerated notion of human potency, while religion admits man's disconfidence in the presence of nature, his helplessness, and his resignation to his destiny. "Both magic and religion are tools of adaptation." Man has tried to adjust himself to his surroundings, to his habits both by magic and religion and will ever continue to do so, though science may correct magic, for knowledge must triumph over pseudo knowledge, and natural causes must supersede occult ones. Yet magic plays its role in society and in its extremely differentiated form, it hinges on beliefs in a mystical impersonal force called, *mana, Wokua* or *bongo*'.

The differentiation between magic and religion becomes still less remarkable in case of primitive men. The Mundas go to the top of hills and throw down stones of all sizes and descriptions, so that the rumbling sound of stones falling would resemble the rumble or thunder and they believe that rains will follow.

Magic also assumes a uniformity of nature as we have seen, and that brings magic in line with science. As Frazer says,

> The magician does not doubt that the same causes will always produce the same effects, and that the performance of the proper ceremony, accompanied by the appropriate spell, will inevitably be attended by desired results, unless indeed his incantations should chance to be thwarted, and foiled by the more potent charms of another sorcerer.

The intimate relationship between magic and religion, while it makes the priority of either difficult to prove, puts a premium on human efforts and initiative. Magic and religion serve the same purpose, viz., that of restoring confidence in times of danger or crises. When magic fails, religion helps, and both may partially contribute towards tiding over social or economic crises. In the normal day-to-day life of primitive man, there may not be any mystery but in his sleep and in times of impending danger, mystery is associated with his experience, so that he combines his fear and hope with the concept of supernaturalism.

This means, as *Marett* has categorically stated that the recognition of the supernatural does not involve a conception of nature; the knowledge of which has been acquired late in the career of the human race, and even today its configuration has not been definitely delimited.

Looking at Frezer's theory from critical angle, we notice, that in fact, the distinction between religion and magic is not so much founded, as Frazer would like us to assume in an essentially different attitude of man toward the entire universe. To Frazer, magic is the direct coercion of natural forces by man: religion is the propitiation of divinites by the believer. The difference between the two, however, is to be found in the subject-matter; religion refers to the fundamental issues of human existence, while magic turns round specific, concrete and detailed problems. In its dogmatic strictures, religion always presents itself as a system of belief defining the plan of man and his goal. As Malinowski has pointed out in criticism, science, magic and religion are differentiated by subject-matter by the type of mental processes, by social organization, and by their pragmatic functions. Each has its own clearly distinct form, science is based on technology, based on observation and contained in the theoretical precepts and later on, systems of knowledge. Magic appears as a combination of ritual act and spoken spell. It is revealed to man not through observation and experiences, but in mythologically founded miracles, religion takes the form of public or private ceremonial, prayer, sacrifice and sacrament.

"Magic, religion and science," suggests Malinowski, "must be examined as active forces in human society, in organized cult and behaviour, and in human psychology."

Durkheim's View of Magic and Religion

The next important view of magic and religion that remains to be examined is that of Durkheim.

Durkheim, as we know, interpreted religion in relation to society. Applying his basic assumption of dichotomy which divides the universe everywhere into "sacred" and "profane", we find that he calls religion – "sacred" -while magic to him is "profane".

Magic and religion to him, are two separate things. It is not merely the spirits and deities in his view, that loom as sacred, but also the impersonal force, which Melanesians – call *mana*. "Durkheim's minimum definition of religion implies an antithesis of the sacred and the profane, and the union of the fellow-worshippers of the sacred in a sort of church -" (Lowie). It is this union into one form of Common-Church, which characterizes religion and distinguishes it from magic, which has no such union.

"There is no church of magic" writes Durkheim. Between the magicians and the individual – who consult him, as between these individuals themselves, there are no lasting bonds which make them members of the same moral community, comparable to that formed by the believers in the same God.

The magician has a clientele and not a church. Durkheim calls magic "anti-social and churchless mockery". For Durkheim, "religion is essentially social", while magic is individual, and even anti-social. This seems largely the reason for his putting them into two categories of sacred and profane respectively.

It should be noted that this distinction would be inapplicable to many of the communities, for example to Frobri and garden magic or to the magical practices connected with the Kuley, as Piddington tells us. In both of these magical systems involve rites which are concerned with the common inspirations of the whole community are inextricably interwoven with those designed to promote the interests of individuals.

Malinowski's Interpretation

A different distinction between magic and religion has been drawn by Malinowski. "Compare a rite carried out to prevent in childbed with another typical custom a ceremony in celebration of birth", he says. "The first rite is carried out as a means to an end, it has a definite practical purpose which is known who practice it and can be easily elicited from any native informant. The postnatal ceremony, say a presentation of a new-born or a feast of rejoicing in the event has no purpose; it is not a means to an end, but is an end in itself. It expresses the feelings of the mother, the father, the relatives, the whole community, but there is no feature event – which this ceremony fore-shadows, which it is meant to bring about or to prevent. This difference will serve us as a *prima-facie* distinction between magic and religion.

While in the magical act the aim is always clear, straight forward and definite, in the religious ceremony there is no purpose directed towards a subsequent event.

The objection to this as basis of classification is that it leaves many of the phenomena "unclassified". Thus though we may agree with Malinowski's formulation as Piddington tells us; as to represent another sight of the fact that religious ceremonies cannot be considered apart from subsequent events, are supposed to follow from their performance on the one hand, or from failure to carry them out on the other.

We can sum up this controversy, agreeing with Piddington, that no attempt to differentiate between religion and magic in primitive communities can be satisfactory. It is a waste of time to attempt to lay down dogmatically what is religion and what is magic, as though there were some pre-ordained distinction between them. Any distinction drawn must rest upon the procedure of abstracting from religion and magic as conceived by ourselves' to contrasting elements which are then applied to the quite different categories of primitive magico-religious systems.

There can thus be drawn no hard and fast line of demarcation between magic and religion.

Concluding Review

After a detailed discussion of magic and religion that so largely attracted our attraction, it becomes necessary to put here a few remarks as the concluding review of the whole subject.

From our discussion, it is clear that magic and religion–both are found existing all over the world, that is to say these are universally practised. Whether magic was prior to religion, or the *vice-versa*, is not yet ascertained, nor does it matter much. The ethnographic evidence available till now has not been able to trace any society where man may have totally given up magical performances and taken recourse to religion completely, nor any society which may have been solely and wholly magical with no religious beliefs and practices. It would thus be illogical to separate magic from religion postulating the priority of one over the other. Societies, both primitive and modern, savage and civilized are found having a faith in magic and religion alike.

Primitive man has not yet been able to make out which of the two is more helpful to him and thus came to conclusion whichever he should give up. Hence he has continued to practice both.

Magic and religion both exist also because they fulfil certain functions to society and are socially useful. Though various primitive peoples have different conceptions of the operation of supernatural forces, of the extent to which these act directly or through the agency of spiritual beings, of the moral justification or the culpability of magical practices, and of the specific power of particular individuals, they all possess a magico-religious system. Very broadly the function of this is to provide psychological safeguards against failure, methods of controlling the incalculable expressions of collective optimism, explanations of failure and disaster, and ways of securing and enforcing socially orientated co-operation.

We do not know how primitive peoples first arrive at beliefs and practices connected with the supernatural. All that we can observe is that they all have such beliefs and practices which are passed on from generation to generation as part of the cultural tradition, and that the existence and vitality of such beliefs and practices depend upon certain universal characteristics of human life. Magico-religious beliefs and practices provide–(a) an explanation of incalculable and uncontrolled events in human life, and (b) a putative way of controlling them and steps which can be taken to express the hopes of human beings concerned and to establish their faith that these hopes will be realized. The function of religion is also to help man to survive; at times of miseries and disasters of his life; it gives him the solace and fills with reassurance by a faith in the almighty. Gods, spirits and high powers are propitiated to secure their help in order to get over the crises of life.

Summing up the whole case, we can maintain that magic and religion–both play their roles in society. Religion and magic both become "tools of adaptation which help man to come over the tensions of life. So far as they are of such help to man they will continue to command his supreme respect and faith.

7

Position of Women in Primitive Society

ALMOST Everyone Understand – What does the question of 'Position of Women' mean. In essence and in its fundamentals, it refers to the status of women which they occupy in our society or in the primitive society. Formerly, and till recently, it was a custom to understand by this a discussion on the inferior status of women which they generally have in most of the societies, often correlated with a suggestion of improvement. But our anthropological knowledge must have enabled us to understand fully that question of inferior status of women does not always and at all places holds true. She is also seen to enjoy a better status more in many of the primitive communities.

To express in the words of Lowie; "Dramatically opposite views are current among the educated laity about the women's place in primitive society. On the one hand, she is conceived as little better than a slave or beast of burden, condemned to perform the hardest drudgery, bought as commodity, and without redress against her most brutalities. But those who have read of tribes, reckoning descent from the mother and have imbibed the shop - worn anthropological doctrines of half-a-century ago are likely to view primitive women as undisputed mistress of the family, if not of communal life as well."

Both conceptions, so far as the overwhelming majority of peoples are concerned, reminds Lowie, fall ludicrously wide of the mark. However, there is so much variability in the relation of woman to society that any general statement must be taken with caution.

To understand women's position in the society, it would be better to approach the subject through a number of different avenues, that is to say by quoting practical examples, before venturing on even a qualified dictum.

Thus before proceeding to deal with the subject further, it would be well to make out the difference between theory and practice.

First of all, it should be noted that the treatment of woman is one thing, her legal status another, her opportunities for public activity still another, while the character and extent of her labours belong again to a distinct category.

This distinction between theory and practice becomes still clear when we consider some well-known phenomena. "The harem beauty is not compelled to perform the drudgery of a menial, yet her position is not consistent with our ideals of human dignity, and the same applies in only slighter degrees to the European lady of quality in the age of chivalry". (Lowie).

In a very different environment, the Toda women. While well treated, rank as inferior and are excluded from the ritualistic observances that occupy the little employment on their hands, being prevented even from cooking, at least whenever the food contains milk as an ingredient. She suffers thus from many of the social disabilities despite the fact of the matrilineal descent.

On the other hand, we find that the Andaman Island woman is virtually on a plane of equality with her husband, though a somewhat larger share of work may fall upon her shoulders.

In Central Asia, comparison of Kirgiz and Altaian conditions is especially instructive. Both tribes assign to women a position of distinct inferiority. The Kirgiz, moreover, possibly under the influence of Islam, treat their wives with much, greater severity than the Altaian Turks. Though superficially, both may seem to occupy the same legal status, but in fact, the social status of the Kirgiz woman is decidedly better, as closer scrutiny reveals. Among the Kirgiz the division of labour is a far more equitable one, for men tend the cattle, secure fuel, make containers, and till the soil. Possibly in consequence of this very fact, the Kirgiz women enjoy a much greater freedom than is granted to their sex in the Altai.

They participate at festive occasions, visit back and for at pleasure, attend games and take part in competitive singing concerts. In short there is ample compensation for the repeated harshness of treatment.

As we find here, the above case illustrates the great caution required in summing up the status of the female sex in a given society. The conditions involved in the relations of men and women are many - sided, and it is dangerous to overweight one particular phase of them. Theory may and does affect practice but often only in moderate degree. Theoretically, the Mohammedan Kirgiz may divorce his wife at will, practically, he very rarely does so.

We should also mention here that Chinese metaphysics associates the female principle of the universe with evil, and the legal status of women is one of abject inferiority. This has neither prevented a family large number of women from establishing their supremacy in the household by sheer strength of personality nor from playing an appreciable part in literature and affairs. If instead of so extreme a case, if we revert merely to the recent periods of Caucasian civilization, we find that American women were not maltreated prior to suffrage and amendments, that disabilities as to holding or administering property have not involved subjection to a husband's will; that at a time in which little was heard of emancipation, the leaders of the Parisian beliefs exerted a social influence hardly to be overestimated. It other words, it is important to ascertain what customary or written law and philosophic theory have to say, is more important to know whether social practice conforms to theory or leaves it halting in the rear, as it so frequently does. The exaggerated weight often ascribed to abstract proportions and legal enactments, is part of that perverse rationalism which has often begrudged the understanding of students of human institutions and human psychology.

Matrilocal Residence and Matriarchate Affecting the Position of Women

The position of women is affected in practice by many others. The matrilocal residence and that matriarchate or where the descent is traced through the mother go in long way in determining the position of women. Naturally where the husband goes to live with his wife at his wife's house or with her parents or kins, the status of women is apt to rise higher than in the societies where she has to live in her husband's house and is treated as a stranger. But we should be cautians not to overestimate the views here with regard to feminine superiority. The immediate result of matrilocal residence is not in fact, feminine superiority, but only the superiority of the wife's kin. Much has been said about mother-right affecting the women's superiority but this would be an overestimation of the facts; though it remains true that her position under matrilocal residence is no doubt for better than in case of patrilocal residence. There is a great difference between the Siberian Eskimo households in which a wife settles with her husband family, and those where the bridegroom goes to his wife's parents. But the difference does not in practice affect the status of woman as woman. In the former case she becomes the subordinate of her mother-in-law; in the latter, she remains the subordinate of her own mother; and in both cases, the supreme ruler is a man, her father or her father-in-law.

It is further clear that matrilocal residence has also a further effect on women's position in another way. Since, matrilocal residence has an effect in limiting the polygynous unions, it also tends to eliminate those difficulties to which a woman is sometimes exposed through conjugal favouritism in a polygynous household. Altogether, then, there can be no question that practically woman profits from continued residence under her parent's roof, even though she has not a free-exercise of her prerogatives – as it is her kins and not she herself that have a hold upon her children and the family. But it should also be noted in the mean time that this need not in the least emancipate her from the thraldom of an alien will. Where the husband may ultimately gain the mastery over the household, (as the case is with the Yukaghir), she will then be in exactly the same position as though she had settled with him from the start.

Under Matriarchate

The question of Position of Women is further understood through matriarchate. It is commonly understood that matriarchate has a greater influence in raising woman's status in society. Some writers are of opinion that the position of women grows more important in the matrilineal societies or those tracing their descent through mother, than in the partilineal societies. At one time, matrilineal set - up was interpreted to mean that women govern not merely the family, but also the primitive community equivalent to the state. Possibly there is not a single theoretical problem on which modern anthropologists are so thoroughly in accord as with respect to utter worthless discussion on the position of women in primitive society.

The testimony of the ethnographic data is too clear to be swept aside by a-priori speculation of the Australians: some tribes are matrilineal, others patrilineal, but the lot of women is not one jot better or more dignified among the former than in the latter. The same holds good for Melanesia as well as for India Many of the tribes in India such as the Todas, the Nayars and the Khasis trace their descent through the mother, but such authority as hers exerts over the children is held not by her but her brother. This results in arancuiate. Thus we see, that matriarchate or the mother-right does not guarantee in all cases, a virtual supreme authority of women, but only an authority is heed by her kins on her behalf. In Africa, we hear of female rulers, but their occurrence seems independent of the rule of descent and no more affects the status of the average Negroes than the reign of Catherine the great affected the position of Russian peasant women.

There are a few instances of matrilineal communities so rare that they can be counted on the fingers of one hand, in which the women either exercise unusual property rights, or play a remarkable part in public life. The Khasi of Assam, the Iroquois and Pueblo Indians furnish the best known illustrations.

Among the Khasi there is a well-nigh unique combination of female prerogative. Here houses, real estate and the prized family jewels are not only transmitted in the maternal line, as is also the case among the Garos, but the authority of the house is held by the women of the maternal line, i.e., these rights descend from mother to daughter. The position of the youngest daughter is very important among the Khasis. She is the custodian of the family property and performs the religious ceremonies. Thus property descends in the female line, and the younger daughter inherits as a trustee for the family. In one locality even the position of the 'pontiff' is held by woman, her success or being chosen for a group of her female kin. Yet it would be grievous error to infer that man counts for 'nought' in Khasis communities. In the household, in spite of feminine ownership, the woman's elder brother ranks as the head of and when the husband, after initially matrilocal residence establishes an independent domicile he is an undisputed lord, moreover the husband's right to kill an adulteress taken – 'iflagrante delicto' is recognised by customary law. Politically the sovereignty is transmitted in the materfamilias–but from male to male member, only where male heirs are wanting, does a woman succeed, and she is in turn, succeeded by her son and not her daughter. This system, thus, we see, is assuredly called 'matriarchal' only by courtesy.

That property considerations have influenced to the structure of social life is common knowledge to field anthropologists. Matrilineal system of inheritance can be traced to the requirements of horticulture and agriculture.

Social needs, such as the performance of religious ceremonies and obligation of mortuary rites have made the Khasi vest the family property in the youngest daughter. Mill has pointed out the complications that have arisen from contacts of the Khasis with the non-Khasis, particularly when the custodian of the family property change her religion, as different interpretations have been put forward by interested parties among the Khasis both Christian and non-Christian. Misconceptions have arisen, as Contille in the "Notes on the Khasi-law" says, due to the fact that occurs, use the legal term 'heir' for the custodian of the property of treating her as the head of a Hindu, undivided family as she really is. The matriliny of the Khasis is associated with the tribal customs prescribing the role of the youngest daughter in family worship and general mortuary rites.

The position of women is also of much status among the Iroquois that furnish the closest approximation to a matriarchal condition. Here the women arranged marriage and probably owned both houses and land. Some of the most important ceremonial organizations were largely constituted and managed by women, from whose numbers there were also taken three of the six ceremonial officials of each sib. Nevertheless it remains a fact that even among the Iroquois no woman had a place in the supreme council of the league.

In Pueblo-villages, we find that the status of women is decidedly less important than among the Iroquois. As Professor Kroeber has well put the case, "It is in the women's ownership of the house that the so-called matriarchate of the *Zuni* centres and rests."

The foregoing cases, then, supply the fortiori basis of the conclusion that a genuine matriarchate is nowhere to be found, though in a few cases, feminine prerogatives have evolved to a marked degree in certain directions. Surely the fact, that such privileges are in a handful of cases linked with matrilineal descent does not warrant the inference that maternal descent is the efficient cause, for the phenomena from Australia, Melanesia, British Columbia, and India, are decisive on that point. Since we have recognised maternal descent itself as the result of more fundamental conditions, such as residence and economic performances, it will be desirable to examine whether these, rather than the descent, have influenced faminine activity and rank. In other words, if there is any causal relationship, the sequence is likely to be not maternal descent, hence matrilocal residence and a certain improvement in woman's juridical status, but rather, matrilocal residence, hence improved status and possibly also maternal descent, and similarly with the other basic phenomena. Thus we find that though matriarchate may furnish a better ground for the position of women, it is not always associated with the superiority scheme in that society. Thus the position is in greater degrees limited.

The Economic Determinant of Women's Position

It is almost an acknowledged fact that economic conditions or economic factors largely determine a social fact. In our own societies we see that how much the position of man is raised in family because of the economic reasons. This remains no less true in case of primitive societies. But one more fact has a greater bearing and that is, that in many of the primitive communities, if not in our modern, women share the burden economically with men in the maintenance of the family.

Since they play an important role in the economic maintenance of the family their position socially is apt to be affected and they naturally assume a better status.

The Sexual Division of Labour

The most important difference, which all cultures must recognize, lies in their respective physiological roles in the reproduction and rearing of children. But this generally leads to a secondary form of differentiation of which the most important in the sexual division of labour. Very broadly, there is a tendency to allocate dangerous tasks and those requiring strenuous and concentrated physical effort for comparatively short periods to men, while relatively safe work, which calls for more prolonged but less concentrated effort, is usually the province of women. A good example of this contrast is to be found in the fishing of the oceanic communities, or the fishing and agricultural work by man in the Muria and Maria communities of Bastar.

In the oceanic communities, we find that deepsea finishing, with its intermittent demand for violent physical effort is the work of men, sometimes sanctioned by taboos on women embarking in sea-going canoes; on the other hand, fishing from the shore and the gathering of sea-food from lagoons and rock pools tend to be the work of women. Very similar is the case with the aboriginals of Bastar–the Murias and the Marias. Among these, Murias and Marias, men are engaged in hunting, fishing, tilling the soil and ploughing the fields, while women help them in harvesting and preparing the threshing floor. They also tend the cattle and are engaged in weeding, gathering fruits and edible plants and roots from forests. In Bastar, collection of forest produce is an important part of the work, mainly and largely carried on by women, who are helped by children. Mat-wearing and basketry-making are solely the women's job while care of the hut doesn't need any particular mention. Thus in Bastar women tend to perform a number of economic activities. This has naturally born an effect on their status which is far better than that of any of their neighbouring counterparts. Among the Australian aborigines the men do the hunting while women father edible plants, fish, or collect, goaennas and other small games.

It is also to be noted that magico-religious functions also determine the position of women in a society. The respective magico-religious functions of men and women are defined in various ways by different communities. In Australia, women are rigidly excluded from the sacred ceremonial of the men, though they carry out other less spectacular rites of their own. In Melanesia, too, we usually find that women play no part in the more important magico-religious ceremonies, which are the exclusive province of men.

It should be noted that in Bastar, the Gond's wife is no drudge to her husband. A certain amount of equality exists between the man and his wife and there is no truth in the general notion that among the primitive tribes all the heavy menial work is as it were thrust upon women and men are a privileged class undertaking only some lighter tasks. Judging all the facts, we may say that the division of labour in these community is fairly equitable. In the division of labour between the sexes, customs and social traditions also play their part.

We may say that generally men play a more important part in magico-religious ceremonial than women but this is frequently offset by the admission of women on equal terms to religious organizations, or alternatively by a definition of different types of religious ceremonial as appropriate to each sex; even though that of the women may be a less specialized job.

A reference to the position of women among the Marias and Murias of Bastar, would not be out of place here.

Among them we find that daughters and sisters in a family have no right of inheritance of their father's or brother's lands or property. For "the land is really the land of the clan", as Grigson tells us, "and the daughters and sisters will on marriage have passed to the clans of their husbands." A widow is entitled only to maintenance, and as after her husband, she very often becomes the wife of this younger brother under "levirate", she gets her maintenance from him as a matter of course, if he leaves no younger brother and does not marry again, she lives on in her late husband's house and works with other women of the family, and she is maintained by their husbands. A girl, if she has no parent's before marriage, goes to a married sister's house and becomes a co-wife (sororate).

For a woman in the Maria society is on the whole a kind of property, or a valuable adjunct to the house and family. For her, the husband's family has had to pay a bride-price that is a severe-tax on its resources, or else, where cross-cousin marriage prevails, she represent the repayment of a debt incurred when her father took his bride from the family and clan to which she goes as a bride. She has to take care for the meals of her husband look after the house, tend the cattle, father roots and plants, she is not a full-human being like her man. She is tabooed . When menstruating, she may not sleep in the field, when the crops are ripening, she is debarred from attending many of the agricultural or first crop-festivals, she has no freedom of movement.

Yet with all this, she has not too bad a position. As a girl, she has considerable freedom, both in pre-marital sexual life and in the choice of a husband, and she is fairly free to leave his husband if he ill-treats her or if he cannot beget a child. Tribal sentiment strongly condemns wife-beating. Her natural taste for ornament is given full scope, her parents gradually collecting feed and metal-neck and arm-rings, her boy companion presenting her with beads and carved hair-combs and her husband when she is married, recognizing her right to spend a few of the scanty piece she earns from the sale of her basketry at the bazaar, or simple trinkets. She participates in the tribal-dances, and songs though not in the religious ceremonies that accompany them.

In fact, her position 'vis-a-vis' her husband, is far free than of the ordinary Hindu-wife. Above all she is not exposed to the evil of child-marriage and pre-mature motherhood of which habits of their Hindu neighbou s Maria headmen will speak with abhorence.

Thus, from our above account, we find, that these economic factors, no doubt, are more prominent in case of primitive communities. Economic factors have probably moulded some aspects of the latter-day civilization and in some schemes of interpretation, they have come to play an exaggerated part. A far-reaching economic change seems bound to produce a modification of some sort in women's life, in her share of work, if in nothing else, as an immediate consequence.

Among the hunting-tribes, like the Vedda and the Andaman Islanders woman contributes only moderately to the commissionary department, yet ranks as man's equal in society. Among the stock-rearing populations, we find, that the status of woman is almost uniformly one of decided and absolute inferiority. Thus it has been shown by some of the writers, that percentage of cases in which woman occupies a low rung in the social scale is

73 among cultivators of the soil, but rises to 87.5 among pastoral tribes. On economic grounds, the matter is readily explained. The domestication of animals was undoubtedly a masculine achievement and practically every where the care of the herds has remained a masculine occupation. But such a complete dissociation of women from productive toil is bound, according to the argument, to lead to her social degradation. In Lowie opinion, this consideration should be extended to agricultural, as distinguished from horticultural tribe.

We thus find a very plausible explanation of the relation of sexes throughout those centres of the old world. Civilization which supplied the basis for our own. We see, why the economically dependent women of China, Central Asia, and India, should be on an unequivocally lower plane than man. In the word of Lowie: "The economic life thus can be a 'causal nexus' of the feminine status". That woman's position in a particular tribe is indeed, a function of the historical relations of the people, becomes clear when we turn to Oceania and Australia. The outstanding characteristic of feminine inferiority in this area are very different from those which impress us in Siberia.

We should also not amiss the fact that a gross consideration of the economic data fails to indicate a particularly close-correlation between them and women's position.

But in view of the current tendency to overestimate the economic motives, it is worthwhile insisting that they merely constitute a co-determinant.

To sum up, we can say, that the economic factors no doubt, have potency, but potency of only a limited kind, liable to be offset by and even negatived by other determinants. There may besides be other factors too having a bearing in determining the status of women folk. Besides this, the physiological characters are also to be taken into account. Child-bearing, menstruation, etc., all have an effect in determining women's status. Most women become pregnant on one or more occasions during their lives, and are subsequently encumbered with young children who are dependent on them for nourishment and attention. Consequently their work is such as is not jeopardized by these necessary biological responsibilities.

The value attached to the economic consideration is perhaps no where more obvious than in case of the Maoris of New

Zealand. This is reflected by the derisive song sung by young people of each sex against the other among the Maoris:

"Who will marry a man
 Too lazy to till the ground for food ? ...."
"Who will marry a woman,
 Too lazy to weave the garments ? "....

One more point should be mentioned here, with regard to the inferiority of women. The indespread practice of polygyny has often been cited as an example of female inferiority. But it is certainly not felt as such by native women. Polygynous households generally run fairly smoothly in the primitive communities at least more so than we would expect them to do, because the rights and obligations of the various parties concerned, are socially recognized. The satisfactory working of a "polygynous" household is greatly facilitated where, as very commonly, the wives are sisters to each other. But we must not build up an idyllic picture of polygynous marriage. In spite of all that has been said, quarrels and clashes of interests between co-wives are far from uncommon, and produce from time to time both social disruption and individual unhappiness. This, of course, is at least partially offset by the fact that, broadly speaking, no marriageable woman is ever without a helpmate or an opportunity to raise a family. Furthermore, in a number of cases, sometimes a woman will actually ask her husband to take another wife in order to heighten her domestic and economic tasks.

Then, we can maintain that the above considerations should lead us to examine very carefully any data brought forward as evidence of 'female inferiority' in primitive society. Though their social role is in general less spectacular than that of the opposite sex, women have their own "spheres of influence" from which they derive satisfactions and rights which are definitely validated in social custom and usage. In the words of Piddnigton: While it would be rash to make any general statement as to whether they are happier or not in our present civilized conditions, it would be more absurd to speak of their "degradation" in primitive society.

It should also be borne in mind that the higher status of women is supposed to be correlated with a higher stage of civilization. In the very simplest hunting tribes, we find that woman is, to all intents and purposes, man's peer. This does not hold for the most of the higher primitive levels, say for the average Bantu village, where woman, though hardly a mere slave, does not at all events, rank as man's equal. Finally on the still higher plane of Central Asia and China, and also in many parts of India, woman is definitely conceived as an inferior being.

To sum up the whole issue, we should remember that apart from theory, primitive woman by force of her personality, and in societies, where as Piddington remarks, "marriage is more practical and less "romanting", is probably as often the ruling spirit of her home as with us. This is equally true in the sophisticated civilizations of China, despite the abstract propositions as to feminine depravity concocted by native philosophers, as well as in India and other parts of the world.

Feminine disabilities such as her monthly course and weaker strength also go to account for her seclusion and inferiority, as found even in advanced communities of India.

Still, in conclusion, we can maintain that neither the superstitious sentiments, nor her physical disabilities, nor man's superiority has debarred the women from the privileges that she enjoys as mother in most of the societies both primitive and advanced.

8

Kinship System and its Importance in the Study of Social Structure

IN All Societies, primtive and modern, some sort of relationship is recognised. This relationship towards kins or relatives is called in anthropological terminology the "Kinship" system. This relationship becomes still more obvious in case of primitive societies.

There are different ways of classifying relatives, blood, parentage, marriage and contiguity of residence are the usual determinants of relationship in human society. Behaviour towards relatives is not the same as behaviour towards non-relatives. "The patterns of kinship behaviour" – writes Hoebel, "are not biologically determined. They are all culturally conceived". Kinship relations consists of the interests roles that are customarily ascribed to the different statuses of relationship by a people. Every culture includes a set of words, or labels, that symbolize each of its kinship statuses. These labels are called Kinship Terms', and the whole is called the System of Kinship (or relationship) terminology of the culture.

Thus kinship-system is the whole process of designating the relationship of the kins by a particular set of kinship terminology.

The first important principle to grasp in the study of kinship systems is that "no system provides a separate and distinct term for every possible kind or position of genealogical relationship."

We note that al systems equate, lump or merge some relatives of different genealogical relationship. For example, the Sema Nagas equate mother, father's brother's wife and mother's sister, the same people use 'apa' to denote father, father's brother – and mother's sister's husband. Again they use 'ani' to denote father's sister, wife's mother, husband's mother, husband's brother's wife. The Comanche Indians equate father, father's brother, and mother's sister's husband all under one term "ap". Father's brother and mother's sister's husband both of whom we call 'uncle' are genealogically distinct from father, but to the Comanche, they are terminologically identical. Similarly one people may call his own son, his brother's son, his wife's sister's son, and his sister's daughter's husband, all by the self same name – (*'tua'*- in case of the Comanche). All these persons are merged or equated under the same identifying term of relationship.

Kinship system in which this practice of merging varians relationships is called 'classificatory systems of relationship'. A system in which each relationship term applies to a particular genealogical status and no other is called 'particularizing' system or 'descriptive system' of kinship. We, for instance, tend to apply the terms "father" and "mother" only to our actual progenitors when referring to relatives.

However, as no system is ever wholly particular we also use certain classificatory terms-such as cousin, uncle, aunt, niece, nephew, grandfather, grandmother, grandson and grand daughter.

Thus we find that there are two principal systems of Kinship terms, one in which the terms are applicable not to single individual persons, but to classes of relatives which may be very large but which are addressed by some common term; and the other, in which terms of address denote single individual person even in the terminology of relationship of most of the Caucasic peoples, which Rivers speak of as the 'family' system sometimes a group of individuals is denoted by one common term, so that the difference in the two systems, classificatory and descriptive, is one of degree only. In the former a term is used to denote a large number of individuals while in the descriptive system of terminology, a term refers ordinarily to one single individual.

The examples of the classificatory types of kinship abound in numbers. The kinship system among the Sema Nagas we have already mentioned above where a kinship term such as 'apu' is used to denote a number of persons standing in different relationships such as father, father's brother and mother's sister's husband. Among the Angami-Nagas, the term 'thi' is used for wife's elder brother, wife's elder brother's wife, mother's brother's wife, father's brother's wife, elder brother's wife, husband's elder sister etc. Among the Hos of Chhota Nagpur, mother's brother, father's sister's husband and the father of both, husband and wife are all called 'poyar'. Again, father's sisters, mother's brother's wife and mother of both husband and wife are denoted by 'hatom'.

It was Morgan, however, who discovered for the first time, the Classificatory System of Kinship. By his studies of the Iroquois where he had worked extensively, Morgan had come to conclusion that all among the primitive peoples, a kinship term may be used to designate a number of persons.

Morgan had showed that among many people, it is assumed that all who live together or make up the home circle are related, and it is considered that other groups are related among themselves in the same way. If the men stay at home, and the wives came from outside, all the men of one's generation, will be called by some term which means "brother", and all the women by a term which means "sister".

Thus Morgan had come to discover that one's own father, his brothers and cousins and even more remotely related men of his generation are called by the same common term which means 'father'. The same thing happens with the other side of the family, the mother, her sisters, cousins on her side, and so on will be 'mothers'. This form of kinship system Morgan termed the classificatory system of kinship since it refers to a number (class) of persons. It is also called the 'Dakota' type of noamenclature after the people among whom Morgan worked and first discovered the system.

Thus, in a classificatory or Dakota type of nomenclature a specific term is used for a set of persons standing in different types of relation and who may even be too remote to be so recognized. The simplest and most highly developed system of all is seen in a Maori village, where all the grand parents generation are grandparents, all of the father's and mother's generations are fathers or mothers, all of the one's own are brothers and sisters, all of one's own generation (children) are referred to as "my children". This is the most developed form of "classificatory kinship system". To quote a few other examples. Tamilian society, mother's brother, father of sister's husband and father-in-law, all are addressed by the same kinship term "Mama" (because of cross-cousin marriage). The Sema-Nagas have a specific term "Angu" to address a number of persons, viz., mother's brothers, mother's brother's children (son and daughter both), husband's father (female speaking) and wife's father (male speaking), husband's brother (female speaking) and wife's brother (malespeaking).

There are various forms of classification in different parts of the world, but in all the classificatory system expresses the extreme solidarity of the group, and the mutual privileges and obligations of the members. Morgan was able to present and analysis in all 139 systems taken from all over the world from whom he picked up his evidence.

As different from these, Morgan showed the other form of kinship system, as prevalent commonly among us and in the western societies, in which a kinship term does not refer to a class of persons, but only to a particular individual, and denotes only a specific relationship.

This he called the 'descriptive' type of kinship system. We speak of uncles and aunts and cousins without distinguishing the side of the family a matter most important to those who have the system which Morgan discovered and named the 'classificatory'. So far, we also use the classificatory 'system of noamenclature, but as kinship system becomes more of 'descriptive' type, as we have more of such words as 'father', 'mother', 'sister', 'brother' etc. all of which have an individual denotation.

The essential characteristics of the descriptive types as defined by Morgan are:

(i) that the terms express actual blood relationship terms. such as father, sister, being only applied to persons having actual blood relationship with the ego speaks,
(ii) that the collateral lines are kept distinct from each other and divergent from the linear, so that the terms nephew and niece are applied to persons related collaterally, the divergence of successive generations being indicated in the names employed,
(iii) that in most cases, except for the nearer relatives, the terms are descriptive, i.e., in these what he believed to be typical and normal forms of the system.

No general terms, like uncle, niece or cousin the person being specifically described as father's brother's or sister's daughter, mother's brother's son. In this system, it should be noted that all the kinship terms refer to the single biological family comprised man, wife and children. Terms for other relations not included in the family are usually vague and indefinite.

The classificatory system, on the other hand, as noted above, reckons kinship between groups rather than individuals, and the collateral lines are not kept distinct and divergent from the lineal.

Morgan, we find, had worked intensively among the Red-Indian tribes from where he had collected much of his data. As early as 1846, while collecting material to illustrate the institutions of Iroquois, Morgan had found among them a system of relationship for the designation and classification of kindred both unique and extraordinary in its character, and wholly unlike any with which anthropologists were till then familiar.

Morgan had also very rightly assumed that 'social reasons' were at the root of the system which he discovered, "but unfortunately in this *Ancient Society* (1877), he passed over a magnificent opportunity to relate these terms to active and observable social causes and proceeded, like the other unilinear evolutionists to develop the family, by a typological series of forms, some of them purely hypothetical" as Penniman tells us.

Morgan also suggested that the kinship terminologies cannot be borrowed, and where similarity between such kinship system is found, he would adduce it to the migration of people from one place to another. Thus in case of much existing similarity between the Tamilian tribes of India and the Iroquo tribe of New York, Morgan would suggest that the former may have migrated to New York.

We find that Morgan's contribution in the discovery of the classificatory system of kinship was original and is of much importance to the anthropological field. By that time nothing was known in this direction, and Morgan by his discovery of such a valuable material indeed made a notable contribution by which later field-work in this direction became possible.

The Chief Categories of Kinship Terminologies

It was further observed after constant study of the subject and field-work that not only social organization but also a variety of interacting factors ultimately determine the form and content of each kinship system. These factors arise from social organization, language, idiosyncrasies, historical contacts and psychological tendencies.

Four decades ago Krober identified eight principles of kinship distinctions that may be seized upon in shaping kinship system. Professor krober, from a comparative study of tribal systems, formulated the principles according to which known systems of relationship are ordered. The chief categories of relationship as conceived by Krober prevailing in the world today, are as follows:

(i) Difference in generation levels: The difference between the persons of the same and of separate generations is recognized, father and grandfather, uncle and cousin are examples.

(ii) Difference between lineal and collateral relationship: The difference between lineal and collateral relationship is maintained. Thus father is distinguished from father's brother.

(iii) Difference in age levels within the same generation: The difference of age within one generation is recognized, as for example, the distinction between the elder and younger brother.

(iv) Difference in sex of relatives such as brother sister, uncle, aunt is recognized. Except for the term cousin, the English terms of relationship are all discriminative of sex.

(v) Difference in sex of the speaker, such as males and females, may have two separate systems of terms. The sex of the speaker is recognized in the terms of kinship. The father and mother may receive one designation from a man and another from a woman. Among the Marathas, a man calls his brother's child 'puṭanya', while a woman calls her brother's child 'bacha'. The Bhotiyas address elder sister as '*pota*' – when a man is speaking and as '*tata*' – when a women speaks; younger sister's husband as '*tete*' – (man speaking), but when a woman addresses him, she says '*poa*'.

(vi) Difference of sex of the person, through whom the relationship is established (father's brother, mother's brother, father's father, mother's father; father's sister's daughter, etc.). In most of the advanced systems, this category is not operative and conventional qualifications are added to distinguish relations, as for example, 'paternal grandfather, and 'maternal grandfather.'

(vii) Difference between genetic relatives and those connected by marriage – (sister, mother, husband's mother etc.). Blood relatives are distinguished from connections by marriage, father-in-law from father, or mother-in-law from mother.

(viii) Difference in status or life condition of the person, through whom the relationship is established.

Thus the distinction in kinship terms is maintained in those used for living and non-living; single or married etc. This is usually not operative in advanced societies.

Few systems make use of all eight distinction but many primitives use the first seven of the eight categories. iii, v, vi, and viii are not operative in English and most European Indo-European languages but the rest are recognized.

The question of the origin of the terminology has been approached from different stand points. Professor Krober claims that descriptive terms are more precise and as in English, restricted in categories, whereas classificatory recognize more categories but express them less efficiently. The purposes to be served by the two systems are the same in each case, and tribal differences are to be explained as matters of psychology rather than sociology.

Professor Krober believes that nothing can be inferred from the particular systems of kinship terms a group uses, and thus the study of kinship system has little practical use. "Kinship terminologies are arbitrary, and unexplainable by any principle other than accident." Against this nominalistic point of view, the terms of relationship which can be deduced from social functions or from particular kinds of marriage are also to be considered.

Rivers had proved that "terms of relationship arise from social functions antecedent to their use."

Thus the 'Hos' use the term *'Hoyar'* to denote mother's brother, father's sister's husband and the father of both husband and wife. The custom of cross-cousin marriage is very much prevalent-among these people and as a result of this form of marriage, the mother's brother and father's sister's husband get to the position of father-in-law, consequently the Hos possess only one term to denote mother's brother, father's sister's husband and the father of both husband and wife for wife's sister, most primitive societies have no special term.

Sometimes it is conventional to address her by a term of endearment or mild reproach as *'sali'* in Bengali. Wife's sister is a potential make and as such a separate term is not required. This has been shown by Majumdar by his study of kinship system.

Importance of Kinship Systems in the Study of Social Structure

The study of kinship-system is not only useful in itself but it also proves of much help in the study of social structure or in understanding the social organization of a people.

In most primitive societies extended kinship groups play larger roles than in the case with us. In such societies, merging or lumping of relatives on a collateral basis, is, therefore, much more likely. Since kinship terms designate social statuses, what we must call a person ideally determines how we must behave towards him. Further all persons who are called by the same kinship term should, (and again ideally) receive the same sort of behaviour, since they enjoy theoretically identical statuses, in the system of social organization.

A native (such as the Comanche) may not only call his father's brother 'father' but also behave towards him as though he were father. He may also call mother's sister 'mother', and behave towards her as though she were a mother. On her part, a women not only calls her own offspring "son" and "daughter" but she also applies these terms to her sister's children. They also call her in return as 'mother'. A man calls his brother's wife as "wife" and behaves towards her as though she were his wife. So also does she behave towards him. Thus in the use of kinship system we find that not only is it reflected in the forms of address or usage.

The kinship system helps us much to understand particular ways of behaviour in a society. They reveal some social reasons to be at the root of a prevailing behaviour.

Where we find that a man calls his brother's wife by the same kinship term which he uses for his own wife and that she might as well get used from the outset to future eventualities. So she responds by calling him "husband", and each calls the other's children "son" and "daughter," though their fates may never bring them together as actual husband and wife. And our study in this case may reveal the fact that these kinship terms in the above case may be in anticipation of levirate marriage in which a man may be entitled to inherit his brother's widow, though in practice he may never be able to do so.

The consequences of sororate are similar. In anticipation of sororate, or as a result of it, a man may address his wife's sister as his own wife.

But although a woman may marry her husband's brother, she may not marry her own brother. The levirate may transform a 'paternal' uncle into a child's father, but never a 'maternal' uncle. Hence, the merging of father and father's brother, but the bifurcation of father's brother and mother's brother. And although a man may marry his wife's sister under the sororate and sororal polygyny he may not marry his own sister. So the sororate may transform a 'maternal' aunt into "mother" but may never accomplish this for the father's sister.

It is also to be noted that "distinctions may be based on the relative ages of the speaker and the person referred." Also, "kinship terminology may differ according to the set of the speaker.

Lewis - Morgan had maintained that kinship terminologies are originally shaped by the social system. Morgan also held that because of the stability of language, archaic terminological patterns outline the social forms that produce them. Thus kinship often survive as vestiges of former usages that have undergone drastic change. He, therefore, thought that he had evidence in the Hawaiian system to support his evolutionary scheme of family development in which primitive promiscuity preceded prohibition of intermarriage of brothers and sisters. Thus when brother and sister were purportedly free to mate, there was no need to separate the maternal uncle from father, for they could be one and the same. All male relatives on the parental generation were, therefore, supposed to be lumped under a single term. There would be no need to distinguish between their children, except for sex, because all cousins could be offsprings of any of these men. Hence, said Morgan absolute generation merging resulted.

But as we have said same where above, not social organization alone but a variety of inter acting factors ultimately determine the content and form of each kinship system. This was the point suggested by Hoebel.

"The kinship structure of any society consists of a number of such dyadic relations, as between a father and son, or a mother's brother and his sister's son", as Redcliffe Brown pointed out. In an Australian tribe, the whole social structure is based on a network of such relations of person to person established through genealogical connections.

As Majumdar has suggested, "Social functions often explain the use of terms, but the use of terms can also determine social relations. All terms of relationship do not result from 'social functions' antecedent to their use". The social function may be the cause as well as the effect of the use of terms of relationship, the latter may be independent of social functions, they may be simple terms of address' arbitrarily and unexplainable as Krober claims.

"When a kinship term does not reflect the current kinship usage", writes Indrawati Karve, "the very disharmony between the word and the usage becomes significant social fact, useful for the construction of the culture-history of a people."

"Few of the social relations of children are pre-determined by 'kinship status' outside the immediate conjugal family. They are thrown into open competition for social status with success and prestige for some, frustration and insecurity for others." (Hoebel).

Summing up the whole case, we can maintain that whatever may have been the strong or weak points involved in the Kinship system, they serve an important purpose in the study of social system and are immensely useful in this way.

9

The Sib and History of Sib

AMONG The Studies of sociology and social anthropology, a concept that holds much importance is that of Sib.

The Sib

Besides the omnipresent family group, we frequently find in primitive societies a type of unit that resembles the family in being based on Kinship but otherwise differs fundamentally from it.This is the *Sib* of the American anthropologists which is, usually among the British anthropologists and in common language, called *Clan*.

Definition

The Sib or clan is most briefly defined as a 'unilateral' kinship group.It is distinguished from the family, which is a bilateral, as it traces kinship from both the sides i.e., father's as well as mother's. To say, that an individual belongs to a certain family implies that he recognizes relationship with a certain man as his father and a certain woman as his mother. Thus relationship in a family is recognised from both the sides. The Sib traces kinship through either parent (either mother or father) to the total neglect of the other.

If a tribe is organized into mother-sibs, called clan by American anthropologists, every child regardless of sex is considered to a member of its mother's sib, and takes the maternal sib name, if there is one. If the tribe is organized into father-sibs called 'gentles' by most American anthropologists, every child follows the father's sib and takes the father's sib name. The other parent, for sib purposes counts for naught, just as in many European countries and also in many parts of India, the mother is neglected as regards the transmission of the family name. The father-sib thus embraces a male ancestor, his children male and female, and the children of his male descendants through males. Correspondingly, the mother-sib includes a female ancestor and her descendants, that is her children and the children of her female descenders through females.

As Distinct from Family

The sib, as we have mentioned above, differs from the family, though it also like the family, strengthens the bonds of relations. Let us here note some of the points of difference between the two:

(i) First of all, as mentioned above , Sib recognises relationship only through one side, i.e., one parent and is thus a Unilateral Kinship group. The family, on the other hand is bilateral, and reckons descent and relationship from both sides, i.e., from both the parents.

(ii) Secondly, Sib has a certain advantage over the family, as it is more compact than the family, while family is a loose unit. Sib is more fixed unit. Divorce and migration rend the family disintegrated but the sib bond is permanent.

(iii) The Sib or clan is also more inclusive, despite eliminating half of the blood-kin, than the family, with respect to the relatives who are recognized.

(iv) Then we note that there may be differences among the relatives, i.e., these treated as blood relatives and other, e.g., brother and sister (blood relatives) father's sister, or father's brothers, children. But there are no such distinctions in a clan, for all members of a clan or sib are regarded as blood-relatives.

Members of a clan have a feeling of consanguity i.e., sameness of ancestry, as they regard themselves to have descended from a common ancestor.

Thus these characteristics of sib organization distinguish it from the family, which is also a kinship group like the former.

Characteristics of Sib

The sib is characterized by its three most common characteristics – (i) exogamy, (ii) Dakota-type of nomenclature, and (iii) the mode of reckoning descent.

Exogamy

Exogamy is the most common characteristic of the sib organization. As mentioned above, members of a sib are regarded as the blood-relatives, hence marriage among them would be incestuous. Sib-mates of the same generation usually call one another "siblings", and from this usage they are a fraternal attitude towards name, it is but a step to the feeling that marriage between sib-mates would be incestuous. This may be largely due to extension of Dakota type of Kinship terminology. Hence, we find as one of the most common traits of the sib, the law of exogamy. The intensity of the sentiment that marriage should be outside the sib varies considerably, but the feeling of exogamy is all the time there. The Iroquois, whom Morgan studied, evince no horror of sib-incest, punishing transgressions with nothing more painful then ridicule, while the Miwok content themselves with pointing out the impropriety of marrying within the sib.

Dakota-type of Kinship Terminology

The second characteristic of the sib-organization is a more or less adoption of what is known as the Dakota type of Kinship terminology. The sense of kinship among sib-mates is associated with a special type of kinship nomenclature, under which the most remote-relatives of one generation frequently regard one another as siblings. The kinship terminology of tribes organized into sibs conforms with extraordinary frequency of the Dakota-type. The co-relation was pointed out by Tylor and more particularly by Rivers, who has shown how well such a kinship accords with a sib-scheme. The alignment of kindred in-sibs goes hand in hand with their alignment in terminology "It is therefore plausible to convert the functional connection into a causal one, and to say that a sib organization produces a Dakota terminology" – suggests Lowie while dealing with this question.

Whatever qualifications may be made as to interpretation, the empirical fact remains that tribes organized into exogamous sibs have a Dakota type of nomenclature one in which collateral and lineal kin on the paternal and maternal sibs, are merged regardless of propinquity.

Mode of Reckoning Descent

As to this point we have referred above that the sib is a unilateral kinship group, and recognizes relationship through either side of parent. A corollary from this follows with regard to the mode of reckoning descent. Based upon the above view, the sibs may be either patrilineal or matrilineal, i.e., recognizing relation through father or mother. Now the mode of reckoning descent depends on the kind of the sib-organization. If a sib is patrilineal, all the children will reckon their descent from the father's side, inherit names from paternal side and also inherit paternal property. Corresponding to this, in a matrilineal sib, the descent of lineages, name, properly etc. would be reckoned from mother's side.

Types of Sib Organization

The Sib is not universally the same. The sib organizations differ from one part of the world to the other. Taking this diversity of the sibs, we may classify them into three main types:

(i) territorially organized,
(ii) totemic, and
(iii) by 'nick-names'.

The sibs may be organized territorially.

They may be spread over a particular territory and all members of that sib may be confined to that very particular area. The Khonds of Orissa are the typical examples of the territorial sibs, which are divided into Gochis which are exogamous units, Similarly the Nagas of Assam are also territorially organized having sub-divisions known as Khels.

The second type of sib, i.e., totemic, are very common. They are organized on a totemic basis, which means that the clan or sib has a particular 'totem' which may be an animal or plant (or some such thing) which is venerated and usually forbidden to and in some cases, is even worshipped. Examples of a number of tribes, organized on a totemic basis can be multiplied in definitely. The Murias of Bastar are divided into sibs on a totemic basis. Thus they are divided into four or five sibs or clans, such as 'Marami', 'Naitam', 'Poyam', 'Sodi', etc., which have their totems in goat, or tiger – ('Sodi having its totem in tiger; and 'Marami, in goat).

The examples of 'nick-names' sibs are found mostly in the American tribes. The crow Indians are divided into thirteen exogamous mother-sibs. These units are designated by nicknames; one is called "They-bring – without-shooting", another "Bad-war-honors", a third "Bad-Leggings" and so forth. Sibmates not only address one another as though they were blood-kindred even when not related, but actually act towards one another as such, gladly giving help when an opportunity offers. Their relations are, however, restricted to the social sphere and do not in any way touch the field of religious activity. The crow were locally divided into a northern and southern branch, but in each were found members of all the sibs.

Thus we find that sibs may be organized into any of these types, or divided into one kind and subdivided into "moeties" or "dual-organizations" in the other type.

We should mention here one more fundamental point involved in connection with the sib-unit. The rule of "once a sib member, always a sib member", suffers hardly any exception as a result of marriage. Almost no case in known whatsoever, according to Lowie in which a man enters his wife's sib; and on the contrary, the only good illustration seems to be that of the Toda, where the wife adopts her husband's sib.

On the other hand, we also find that adoption plays a more important part. When a man adopts a child, then in a patrilineal community it becomes automatically a member of his sib, and in a matrilineal community of his wife's sib, just as that he would be a real child.

Functions of a Sib

The Sib also fulfils a number of functions, though these vary from place to place. Let us examine some of these functions with the help of some concrete examples:

The Hopes sibs of northern Arizona are matronymic and exogamous, father and son are never in the same sib; hence a father cannot pass on his ceremonial privileges to his own child, but transmits them to his nearer sib relatives, his brother's and his sister's sons. It is in this manner for instance, that leadership in the Snake fraternity continues to be inherited. The tremendous role of ritualism among the Hopi thus colours their sib concept and sharply differentiates it from that of the crow, where sibs ceremonies are quite dissociated.

The multifarious functions with which the sib may be invested and the complexities of which this type of organization is capable are well illustrated by the 'Winnebago' of Wisconsin. here we encounter in the first place, what is known as a "dual organization" in which the entire tribe is divided into two Sibs or two "halves" as they can be conveniently called, which in this case are patronymic. These two father-sibs are exogamous like the more numerous sibs of the crow and Hopi. They are symbolically connected with the sky and the earth, one group being called 'those above' and the other 'those on earth. Besides regulating marriage through the rule of exogamy, these sibs play a part on the warpath, in ball-games, and in one of the tribal feasts, for on all these occasions, individuals are grouped according to membership in the two sibs.

The information given about various sib-organizations of the world, furnishes us with the view that the functions of sibs are subject to variation. These examples should suffice to elucidate the diversity of function that may be associated with a system. The sib thus appears as an extraordinarily changeable social unit. It is commonly exogamous but is sometimes only derivatively so as the 'Winnebago'. It may be linked with animals and plants towards which a definite attitude is prescribed, and it may be wholly divorced from any such connection. It may also be a local, or a non-local unit, a political or non-political division of society. Thus a sib may take over important and a large number of functions or remain content with a few. This variability suggests an important problem.

Sibs in Higher Order

Let us now see what the sibs in some higher order are. Morgan had pronounced for the priority of the sib-organization and emphasized it over and again. Morgan pronounced exclusively in favour of the course of development in the social evolution, and as Lowie remarks: "it must be confessed that there is a good deal to be said on behalf of his theory. It has considerable *a priori* plausibility, nothing seems simpler than that an increasing sib should split up into segments retaining a certain cohesion." Further, as Morgan has pointed out, there are instances of the larger aggregate bearing the name of one of the its sub-divisions and also of lesser sibs representing different species of one genus designating the greater division.

It should be noted here that by far the most interesting type of major sib is the moiety, though it also occurs as a simple undivided sib, as among the Miwok and Yokuts of Central California.

There is a peculiar fitness in the association of the Dakota type of kinship nomenclature with a sib-organization. But that fitness is specially marked when the sibs appear in the form of moieties. Certain features of the Dakota terminology would harmonize in equal degree with any sib system regardless of the number of units.

Besides explaining the Dakota-type of nomenclature a dual organization is certainly the simplest that can be conceived. Among the Todas of Southern India, the moieties are endogamous but subdivided into exogamous father-sibs so that each Toda moiety corresponds to the whole of an 'exogamous tribe. Now within the Teivaliol moiety, which embraces six sibs, the one named Kuodr is numerically preponderant to such an extent that in order to observe exogamy its members have married nearly all the available members of other sibs, leaving very few of these to intermarry with one another. Rivers recorded 161 marriages between Kuodr people and the rest of Teivaliol as against 16 members of the other five exogamous groups. Owing to the enormous development of one clan (sib), the Teivaliol division has almost come to be in the position of a community with a dual marrying organization in which every member of one group must marry a member of the other group, but there is no reason whatever to think that this is due to any other reason than the excessive development of one clan (sib) in number.

After a thorough discussion Lowie does not agree with the theory that moieties were necessarily or even frequently the most ancient representatives of a sib organization. That the dual organization accords better with the Dakota terminology than other forms of sib organization is no reason for assuming its uniform priority in contravention of the facts of distribution and definite evidence of the secondary origin of moieties.

Totemism and Sibs

Not infrequently the sibs bear the names of animals and plants, other natural phenomena terms sometimes, though far more rarely, are also substituted. This mode of designation is fairly often coupled with beliefs and practices revolving about the eponym. Frequently, there is a belief in the descent of the sib from the eponym. All these and similar usages are brought together under the head of 'totemism' and the animal, plant or object in question is called a 'totem'. Thus we find that very often the sibs are associated with totemism, and the two go together, go together, though this may not be invariably or necessarily so always as a rule.

Totemism has a very wide distribution, being found in America, Australia, Melanesia, Africa and parts of Asia. Associated with this there runs an idea in some quarters that totemism everywhere is essentially the same, though this view is generally not agreed upon.

As Lowie has suggested in "this connection: "The association of animal names with sibs is one problem and where it appears in a continuous area as in the Eastern United States, its historical implications are obvious; there has been a borrowing of a mode of sib designation". That sibs fairly often taboo the eponymous animals is a phenomenon of great psychological interest which well merits study. But only confusion can result from envisaging what is disparate under a single head.

History of Sib

There has been a hot controversy on the subject among the

writers as well as among the social anthropologists with regard to the origin of Sibs. A number of theories have been put forward to account for the origin of sibs, and some even to dispute the priority of family. One such important theory is that of Morgan, which primarily disputed the claim of the bilateral family.

Morgan's Theory

It was Morgan who first of all largely fought for the cause of sibs. Morgan's study of some of the North American Indian tribes had impressed him so much with regard to the sib-systems that he was almost convinced that sib was the most primeval and universal institution which even preceded the bilateral kinship group the family. Morgan held that the family was a late product which had been almost uniformly preceded by the sib. In his scheme the 'exogamous sib' represents a remarkable reformatory movement that retrenched the intermarriage of blood relatives, gained a foothold through the biologically beneficial results produced thereby, and spread in consequence over an enormous area. In this theory two elements require examination – the alleged effects of the sib system, and secondly, its pretended distribution. It is on these two formulations that Morgan's whole theory of sibs is based. We will examine in brief the validity of these arguments.

As to the first argument we can object by saying that apart from the fact that modern biological opinion is by no means agreed as to the necessarily evil results of inbreeding, there are certain obvious difficulties in the way of Morgan's interpretation.

What Morgan may fairly be criticized for is his failure to realize that exogamy does much more than prescribe the marriage of brothers and sisters: it precludes sexual relations between certain cousins of the most remote degree of propinquity, nay, even between wholly unrelated sib members while in no way interfering with the relations of even first cousins who are not of the same sib. Cross-cousin marriage is perfectly consistent with sib exogamy; but so are also marriages between certain parallel cousins. What the sib, then really does, is to bar incidentally the union of certain close kinsfolk along with that of remote and putative kindred, while permitting the marriage of certain other relatives.

The second assumption of Morgan as to the practically universal occurrence of the sib in primitive society requires more extended scrutiny.

Contradicting or refuting this basic assumption of Morgan's scheme, Lowie endeavours to establish the counter-proposition that the sib is lacking precisely among the more primitive tribes and as a rule appears only when horticultural or pastoral activities have partly or wholly superseded the chase as the basis of economic existence; which is to say in other words, that when a tribe passes from hunting to the pastoral or agricultural stage. Ethnographic evidence shows that most of the primitive tribes in many parts of the world lack the sib-organization.

From this, as Lowie suggests, there directly follows the chronological priority of the family. When we find many of the tribes whom we can list among the most primitive ones are lacking in the sib-organization, but are having at the same time the family, does this not serve as a proof of the priority of family over sib? Moreover, family is found to exist in all parts of the universe, under all conditions and in all times, and from this, we naturally come to the conclusion that family is prior than the sib, and that the sib is only a late product. Thus Lowie points that hence if we really find the family present and the sib lacking in the lowliest cultures as almost exception, we shall obey to the dictates of reason in concluding that the family is an earlier and the sib a later development.

This scheme of Morgan was severally challenged by Swanton who is regarded as "the first who threw down the gauntlet to the current dogma by a trenchant application of the principle of cultural appraisal." Swanton showed conclusively that virtually all the ruder (American) Indian cultures lacked the sib scheme; while the sib appeared among tribe with a far richer, economic, industrial, ceremonial and political equipment. Thus the immense sibless region of northern California, Oregon, Washington, Idaho, Nevado, Utah and all of north-western Canada, save a few, represents uniformly the lowest grade of human existence on the continent.

The reason why Morgan failed to notice this is laid largely in the fact that he being a New Yorker, commenced his researches among the Iroquois, thence proceeding westward through the zone in which the sib organization was dominant. In his time the Indians of the Far East were almost completely unknown for ethnographic purposes, hence his generalization that all North American tribes had sibs was pardonable. Had he begun his work in Oregon or Idato, his entire scheme would presumably have been different. Thus, we find "the fault lies largely in a matter of chance". But at the same time it should be taken into view that "what was excusable in 1877 is no longer so forty years later"; and "while a premature conclusion as a result of partial ignorance is but a venial blot on the master's escutcheon, its tenacious championship today must 'blight' the scientific reputation of the epiganoi."

The ethnographic evidence at our disposal further shakes the conviction of the priority of sibs over family. We find that the North American data do not necessarily agree with the phenomena observed elsewhere. Turning to the southern half of the New World, we find that the lowest culture, that of the Tuegians, is again characterized by the lack of a sib organization. In Asia the evidence is especially only suggestive. Sibs are typical of the Turki peoples, who possess highly developed system of stock-raising and are renowned for their skill as metallurgists: but they are wanting among the Chukchi and Koryak. In India, the Nagas, the Gonds and the Khasi of Assam, horticultural and tinctured with the political notions of a higher civilization, have sibs. Most convincing of all is the fact that the Andaman Islanders of the Negri in the Bay of Bengal, who are supposed to be one of the oldest people of the earth, are untouched by the waves of enlightenment that carried iron and horticulture even to the remote Philippines are devoid of the sib institution.

In case of Australia, we find that in the island continent the sib is a widely diffused institution and presumably an old one. But this does not involve the admission that it is older than the family, for here, as elsewhere we do not find the sib without the family, but both institutions side by side.

Hence the utmost that can be conceded is, that in Australia, the problem of priority remains indeterminate. Even were it otherwise, the Australian data would prove nothing for the sequence of stages in other regions for the Australian culture is by no means more primitive than that of the Paviotso or Andaman

Islanders. In short, we can say, that with one notable exception of the Australians, the simplest cultures lack the sib and possess the family, and even in Australia there is no evidence that the sib is more ancient than its invariable concomitant.

One more point be mentioned here.The position that cases of lacking sibs are not due to recent disintegration of native customs can be rendered impregnable with the aid of the heavy artillery of kinship nomenclatures. As an empirical result there has been a determined correlation between the sib organization and the Dakota type of kinship terminology, that which distinguishes maternal and paternal relatives in the parents' generation but merges kindred regardless of 'degree of relationship'.

It should be, then conceded, that it is relations of the narrow family circle, that are primary, and there has simply been a secondary extension in attenuated form to wider and wider circles of real and putative kin. In Australia, as elsewhere, the family is basic, and primary, the sib relatively unessential and a secondary development. The reversal of the traditional sequence is, in Lowie's opinion, "one of the softest conclusions of modern ethnology."

The Origin of the Sib

Now the question arises – how did then the sib originate on the basis of earlier family concept. In setting out to answer this querry,we must recollect what the sib really is. The sib, as we have seen, is a group of 'selected' kin, and the problem is – hence comes the principle of selection. Why are certain relatives put together to form a 'social unit' to the exclusion of other kin?

As Lowie suggests, the transmission of property rights and the mode of residence after marriage must have been the most effective mean of establishing the principle of unilateral descent, and they might originate both a patrilineal and a matrilineal community.

Among the Hupa, we find that the residence with them is patrilocal, but not quite definitely so. That is to say, in the majority of cases, the paternal grandfather, father, son and son's son of a man are natives and occupants of the same village, taking their wives from without. In other words, the Hupa system actually unites by residence those male relatives who are united in a 'father-sib'. We have here the germ out of which a father-sib might readily develop. When the principle of patrilineal reckoning is once established in this fashion, the residence rules may decay without affecting the system since a man's membership is fixed once and forever by the group appellation.

Professor Speak's intensive researches among the north eastern Algonkian peoples demonstrate the joint action of contigious residence and common property rights.

We also note that the explanation offered for the segregation of patrilineal kin may in corresponding fashion be applied to the assemblage of matrilineal kin. In this connection, Tylor has urged the importance of matrilocal residence. Obviously, whenever the bridge comes to reside permanently in the house of his parents-in-law, the children will as a matter of course be associated with his wife's rather than with his people. It has been shown that this is the natural correlate of anomalous matrilocal unions even among a predominantly patrilocal tribe like the Hupa. But influence of matrilocal residence appears most clearly in such cases as those of the Hopi and Zuni, where there is not merely matrilocal residence but hereditary transmission of the house from mother to daughter, Grandmother, mother and daughters are thus united into the core of a social limit, and all children, born in the house are invariably linked with this permanent group.

From the points of view here assumed, it is intelligible why a considerable number of tribes should lack a sib-system, since unilateral reckoning of kinship is found to depend on certain special usages such as a definite rule of residence, which are common, but not universal; and further because there may be a conflict of mutually exclusive unilateral principles, yielding the palm to neither. On the other hand, the frequency of the sib institution seems roughly to correspond to the wide distribution of the causes here reckoned with. Finally, the multiple origin of the sib, which was previously suggested on other grounds, is rendered still more likely, if anything underlying the sib phenomena such as the residence rule or inheritance law. For in these rules lay the possibility for an indefinite number of independent development of patrilineal matrilineal descent.

Before concluding, let us make a note here that Tylor accounts for the origin of sibs in the matrilineal form, which later passes to the patrilineal. He supports his argument by pointing towards the geological evidence, in which he finds, in the fossils of the period, proof for the matrilineal priority. Applying his triple stratification, he collected with these layers certain primitive usages, such as couvade and draws from their presence in some and absence in others, the far-reaching conclusion of matrilineal priority. But it should be remembered that this is also a one-sided case. To posit the priority of matrilineal sibs over the patrilineal would be as illogical and subject to some criticism, as to posit the priority of the later over the former. (i.e. vice-versa). A more logical solution to this problem seems in the suggestion of "a parallel development" of both the types of sibs, without the necessary for the priority of one or the other.

Summing up, we can say that there is no fixed succession of maternal and paternal descent; sibless tribes may pass directly into the matrilineal or the patrilineal condition. If the highest civilizations emphasize the paternal side of the family, so do many of the lowest; and the social history of a particular people cannot be reconstructed from any generally valid scheme of evolution but only in the light of its known and probable cultural relations with the people who make a society.

10

The Youth Organization in India and the Institution of Ghotul in Bastar

ONE Characteristic Which distinguishes the primitive societies is their possession of the youth-clubs, which are commonly called the "bachelor's dormitories". Though they are not invariably found in every society, they are usually common in many of the primitive societies.

The youth organization is usually a meeting place or a club of the youths of the community, or the village where all the youths of a community, or tribe in some cases, both the boys and the girls meet, play and sleep together. These are the features commonly associated with a youth-organization wherever found.

It is indeed a curious thing for the anthropologist to find such an institution and still more curious to study it in the light of its historic origin and functions which it fulfills. Before proceeding to discover its origins, let us say a few words, about its position, i.e., as it stands as an institution in the society, through a detailed discussion on this will follow towards the later part of our discussion, while examining its working in the different primitive communities.

This institution of the youth seems to suggest that it exists as a social institution fulfilling certain functions of the tribe or community. It may be that at present it may have left very few functions to discharge, but it may have been endowed with a much heavier responsibility in the past.

The Origin of the Institution

The writers on social anthropology have given various suggestions for the origin of the institution of the bachelor's dormitory. Let us examine these common views in the light of factual evidence at our hand.

Looking for the relevant fact, which seem to have a bearing on the origin of this institution, we find that the distribution of this institution among hunting and nomadic tribes is extremely significant.

1. This institution is most commonly met with in the hunting or pastoral tribes. This gives birth to some suggestions. The need of protection of the community against the raids from outside seems more in the most primeval or the "rudest" people.

The possibility of raids to take away the women is greater in these nomadic or pastoral tribes. This calls for the aid and help of the youths of the village or community, which can be best and easily available if they are kept together. The youth-organization in a community is thus a "stock-energy" of the whole community in "reserve" which can be utilised at times of crisis.

2. The keeping together of the women (commonly the girls of the village) in these dormitories, in many cases also indicates towards the same fact, i.e. of protection of the women of the community, as according to upholders of these views, the women of the village are most safe with the protection of the youth-power.

The existence of the youth-organization is much due to its origin in the causes rooted in what has been said above while it is also strengthened by some more evidences furnished by the anthropologists and writers on the subject.

As D.N. Majumdar suggests while discussing this institution in his *Races and Cultures of India* :

3. The need for protection of the tribal group from the ferocious denizens of the forest as well as from the alien and hostile groups who may prey upon them for women or cattle or for both seems to have a larger hand in the factors leading to the origin of the institution. The ablest hunters of the tribe had, therefore, to be kept together for this purpose.

There must have also been the need of keeping awake during the night or major part of it for purposes of protection. These people usually take rest in the early hours of the night and during the day time which make possible for the dormitory life with its nightly bonfires and its varied programmes of fun and festivities.

One more fact be noted here in this connection. Sex acts are usually tabooed during the busy agricultural season, when men work strenuously in the fields or go on ceremonial hunting in the forest, the women, therefore, have to keep together for some periods of the year as any violation of this has disastrous effects on the economic life of the family and the social group.

Besides this, from the time new crops shoot into corn, and till the harvesting is over all the men sleep apart from their wives in their fields while the latter sleep in the village. This also leads to the compulsory segregation of the sexes. Among the Murias and Marias of Bastar, who have characteristic dormitories, husbands are not allowed to sleep in the house with their wives, so long as the navel cord of the new-born child does not fall. In many primitive societies, e.g. again among the Murias wives have to live separate for three to five days either in the communal hut or any special one provided by the family, during their monthly period when it is taboo to see them, and associate with any body not so polluted. It is also noted among many of the primitive societies that sexual relationship is not allowed between husband and wife during the first few years after child birth, or till the child weans.

Among the Murias and the Hill Marias, sexual relationship within the house is regarded as improper and they go to forests for it. The sanction for this custom, in Majumdar's view, may be traced to the belief that such irregularities result in damage to crops by pests or in other complete loss of yield and general domestic calamities such as excessive precipitation, in adequate rainfall, disease of cattle and crops and the various epidemics which claim their toll from the people.

It is also found that most of the hunting communities which possess the dormitory institution are very sparing in the construction of houses. A family usually possesses one hut which may be partitioned to accommodate cattle or for housing the ancestral shades. Husband and wife sleep in one room with immature children, and when latter grow up, they need to be removed, and wherever the dormitory house exists they are conveniently shifted into it.

From all this we know, institutions can be traced to simple beginnings, and also to a single source. This monogenist attitude the anthropologist appears to have inherited from the biological science, in which anthropology is deeply rooted. Recent researches do not prove the legitimacy of the monogenist view of evolution as it had been found that when history began men found themselves already possessed of those characteristics of skin color, hair form and the shape of the head, which serve as the marks of race.

We should also note, that the origin of an institution, a custom or a religious rite may be an accident, as inventions usually are, but the complicated machinery of social formation that we have inherited today has gathered its complexity and momentum in course of career. Once a particular idea or a custom is introduced by an individual and is adopted by the social group for utility or for a particular effect, it would be kept alive and strengthened by ideas and sentiments not in themselves adequate to start the customs. Such is the case with most of our social institutions.

Thus an institution, may be introduced by accident. The belief in its efficacy may keep it alive in an unchanged form. "The survival value of an institution," as Majumdar suggests, is in proportion to its utility, as every cultural form is an instrument of adaptation.

Its role is to render the process of adjustment of the group to its milieu, as also of the intra-group adjustment smooth and easy.

Thus an institution, may survive through the principle of graded utility. This is how the dormitory institution like that of Bastar, appears to have survived.

With this consideration we come to have some definite idea about the dormitory institution.

The dormitory is a group organization. Its origin may be traced to the compaigns where the ablest hunters of the community took their shelter for purposes of defence and protection of the weaker members, but, in course of time, other traits slowly may have been woven round, and the elaborate Ghotul of the Murias is the past. With a settled life, and a better control of food supply, predatory execursions of neighbouring groups for women or for cattle becomes rare, but economy of accommodation in the house, helps to maintain this communal organisation, as the members find it a convenient place, where to sleep in, and also find a venue for their communal activities. Association of men and women in the dormitory helps to make the group life vivid and concrete. Opportunities for inter-communication between the members of the group set up a group standard of social life and the effects of deviation from the group are seen more in their perspectives.

It is in the dormitory that a system of discipline may be rigorously tried and the success in this direction has contributed not a little to tribal and clan solidarity and apparently sober compliance to traditional usages as we find in most of the primitive groups. Training of boys and girls in the usual economic pursuits characteristics of the group, in social and ceremonial duties, in sex and association matters is inculcated through the dormitory organization and thus the latter fulfils an important role in the tribal life of the community concerned. Above all, the dormitory institution where it exists, ensures tribal endogamy by controlling the movements of women within the tribal area and prohibiting social intercourse between men and women-belonging to different tribes. How far this has been achieved or not depends on the effectiveness or otherwise of the dormitory organization.

Thus we find that the institution of bachelors' dormitory exists largely because of social reasons rooted deeply, and the functions which it fulfil even to this day are as a social institution.

The Youth-Organization in India

Now let us discuss some of the youth-organizations scattered among the various tribes in India.

The institution of village dormitory is found among most of the aboriginal tribes of the Chhota Nagpur plateau, viz., among the Mundas, the Hos, the Oraons and the Kharias. It is also found in Madhya Pradesh, among the Gonds and the Bhuiyas. Most of the Naga tribes in Assam, the Aos, the Memis, the Zhota, the Angamis, the Semas, the Chang, the Konyak tribes of the Naga Hills, and the Kukis possess this institution. Many of the tribes of Melanesia and Polynesia are also known to own such dormitories.

The Mundas and the Hos call it "Gitiora", the Oraons calls it *Jonkerpa* or *Dhumkuria*, the Bhuiyas, "Dhangarbassa", the Gonds know it as *Ghotul*". The Aos and Semas call it *Morung*. All young bachelors of a Munda *tola* or village have a fixed common dormitory in the house of a Munda neighbour who may have a hut to spare for the purpose, while the unmarried girls of a village sleep together in the house of a childless Munda couple, or in the house of a Munda widow. The girls are taken care of by an elderly matron of the village who exercises a general supervision over their morals.

Among the Oraons we find that the bachelors of an Oraon village select together during night in the local dormitory, known as the "Dhumkuria", which is generally situated at the outskirt of a village. There is also a separate house for the girls where the latter pass the night under the guardianship of an elderly duenna. In case a house is not available for the purpose, the girls are distributed among the houses of widow. The Hos also, like the Oraons, have two houses, one for the unmarried young men and the other for the maiden of the village. But the girls are often distributed among the houses of widows.

Many Gond villages in Chhatisgarh region of Maunya Pradesh, have a large house near the village where unmarried youth and maidens collect, dance and sing together at night. Some villages possess two, one for boys and one for the girls. This, however, largely depends upon the prevailing practice or the custom. Usually the Murias among them have a common dormitory in every village, for the village boys' and girls, while the Marias generally maintain separate houses for each.

Among the Angami Nagas, however, the Morung is not always resorted to by the bachelor's, but is used on occasions of ceremonies and "gennas" (pollution).

The Marias of Bastar have a *Ghotul* in every village, but the boys and girls do not always share the same house, as among the neighbouring Murias usually of Kondagaon and Narayanpur in Bastar.

The *ghotul* institution appears to have developed to perfection in some Muria villages, where it has effectively superseded tribal or clan organization. In the Muria *ghotul* the boys and girls who share the same Ghotul are not all of the same clan, and unions of boys and girls there, when they develop into permanent friendship, may end in marriage, if necessary. "This is possible", as Majumdar has pointed out, "because both among the Murias of Narayanpur and those of Kondagaon, among whom the institution is very highly developed, the villages are not scattered like those of the Hill Marias, and several clans share the same village." We will discuss this institution of *ghotul* later at length, in all its perspectives known to us.

We find from our study of the dormitory organization, that life in the dormitory is associated with many customs and observances. Some of these have a traditional antiquity, others have been added in the course of their experience of the functioning of the institutions. Tribal groups living around urban centres are gradually abandoning their customs and practices. Those, for example, that did not possess separate houses for the girls, are having such houses built. The Christian villages have, as Dr Majumdar reports, lately resorted to girls' dormitory with an aged dame in the charge.

Thus, we find that these indigenous organizations are finding it difficult to keep intact their shape and form in toto against the forces of civilization.

The Institution of "Ghotul" in Bastar

The institution of youth-organization has reached a degree of so much perfection in no other part of India, perhaps, as in Bastar in Madhya Pradesh.

The *'ghotul'* as it is called in Bastar among the Murias or the village dormitory, is an interesting and useful social institution among them.

A bachelor's house or an-unmarried girls' house is a common dormitory - among the primitive people of both India and abroad.

The ghotul in Bastar is a bachelors' dormitory being common for both the sexes, among the Murias, and separate for boys and girls among the Marias. Among the Hills Marias of Bastar, there are dormitories which are used by the bechelors and the married men and also by the boys, but in no case are women or girls allowed to visit these houses or huts. Among the Murias living near about Kondagaon and Narainpur in Bastar there is one house, in every Muria village, which is used as dormitory by both unmarried adolescent boys and girls, as we had occasion to witness ourselves during our field-work period in Bastar.

It must be pointed out in this connection that this kind of institution is not to be found among the Gonds of Mandla, Betul, Balaghat, Chhindwara and other districts of Madhya Pradesh. Among the 'Gaitra' Gonds of Chanda, we find separate barracks for bachelors and unmarried women and there is a third dormitory which is exclusively reserved for the use of the married couples of the village.

The Muria Ghotul appears to have attained some degree of perfection, and in many villages this institution has definitely superseded other kind of tribal organization. The Ghotuls have also been found to exist in the Kanker tahsil of Bastar (formerly a separate state) which lies just adjacent to Bastar, on the border of Raipur district on the other side. About this Ghotul institution, Russell and Hiralal in their *Tribes and Castes of the Central Provinces and Berar* published long before any of the work on these tribes was known, write thus: "Many Gond villages in Chhatisgarh and the Tendatory States have, what is known as *Ghotul* ghar. This is a large house near the village, where unmarried youths and maidens collect and dance and sing together at night. Some villages have two, oyne for the boys and the other for the girls. In Bastar, the boys have regular organization, their captain being called Sirdar, and the master of the ceremonies, Kotwars, while they have other officials bearing the designation of the State officials.

From the above account, it is clear that the authors are of opinion that these *ghotuls* are also to be found in Chhatisgarh, but they can be said to be right so far as by this they mean the Muria and Maria habitations of Bastar who are found to possess this institution for no other tribes of the region, such as Gandas, Gadbas, Pankas, Halbas etc., had it, as we verified in course of our tribal survey there for more than a period of four months.

The *ghotul* in Bastar is usually situated at one extremity of a village street in small Muria villages like Palari about three miles from Kondagaon inhabited by the Murias. A big village like Baniagaon, eight miles from Kondagaon, has about hundred Muria families belonging to various totemistic clans. We found that the institution is situated in thickly shaded corner at some distance from the settlement. In Baniagaon there were found two *ghotuls* one in each 'para' 'hamlet' or part of a village each meant for both boys and girls in common.

Looking for the historical perspectives of this institution, we can say that it appears that at the beginning, the dormitories were intended to accommodate all the able-bodied male members both bachelors and married of the village, and to stand in absolute readiness to defend the village against enemies and wild beasts; the women and children living in a more secure and protected area. But in course of time, very many other traits may have been adopted and woven round the dormitory, and as a result of all these, we have the elaborate *ghotul* organisation among the Murias.

It would be worth noting that settled life and better means of food supply do not encourage predatory habits and thus the playing of neighbouring villages and cattle or women have become almost unknown.

But these must have been among the main factors that led to the growth of this institution, and which being added with certain other traits, have caused its survival even to the present day.

The problem of accommodation is also a major one in the small huts of these tribes, and this is a problem which yet remains to be solved. The grown-up members find it convenient to use the dormitory for sleeping and for communal activity. This separating out of the grown up members of the family extends the force accommodation of married couple, and for this convenience sake also, the people may have helped to the growth of the institution in a village.

As Indrajit Singh, in the chapter on the youth-organization, in his *Gonds and the Gondwana*, maintains: "With the establishment of security of person and property and growth of individualism and exclusiveness, the married couples have begun to set up separate establishments and the unmarried only are left in possession of the dormitory".

But there may have been still deeper social reasons which may have necessitated growth of this institution.

As we know from our study of the primitive societies, sex is no horror to native but rather the primitive people prefer some sort of pre-sexual training on the part of both the individuals united to make their married life happier and healthier. Thus this need of special training for each sex under different local and tribal conditions may have led to the existence of such an institution. Besides this the taboo on sexual intercourse before the communal hunt, during sowing, reaping and harvesting operations which have some sort of operations attached to them, must have contributed towards keeping alive the institution of the dormitory though it originated in a period of struggle with the forest, wild animals and alien men. The *ghotul* did not originate from a desire to effect separation of the sexes, as has often been assumed, and as might have been the case, actually with the Maria *ghotuls* of Bastar, or the tribes of Assam.

On the other hand, we find that the Muria *ghotuls* are institutions which serve to provide opportunities for young men and women to stabilize and strengthen intimacies which may be a preclude to marriage. "Thus in the privacy and shelter of these bechelor's houses or dormitories, liasions seem to be the rule rather than exception and obtain sanction of tribal custom," to quote Indrajit Singh.

It should not be lost sight of, however, that this sort of free mixing of young people, and of marital apprenticeship through long courtship and trial intimacies within the dormitory, serve to give the right direction to the sexual urge and lead to happy enduring unions. In this way it affords an easy solution to the marriage problem. Young girls freely choose their husbands here, which have greater probability of making their married life happier afterwards than unselected and chance betrothals. Thus we find that the *ghotul* institution serves as a social necessity in the Muria society besides fulfilling its other role.

The Muria ghotul is usually a long rectangular shaped house with only one big hall, the walls being made of wattle and plastered with mud and rinsed with a solution of either cowdung or coloured clay. There is a big *agana* or courtyard in front of the *ghotul* between the house and the other fence, which usually serves the purpose of a playground in winter and summer when various outer games are played there. It also provides the place for ceremonial dances when the whole of village collects to watch the much celebrated play. During the very hot summer, the members also sleep on the floor. There is usually a fencing of bamboos or woods around the *ghotul* house.

The *ghotul* house has only one entrance, which is at the front. The *ghotul* hall is very compact from the inside. The inside of the *ghotul* and its roof are all covered with soot, the result of burning fire for years inside during winter and rainy months to keep it warm. The hall thus becomes very suffocating with the burning of fire. A few minutes' stay in one of these *ghotuls* is more than enough to make us remember what it is like all through our lives. The *ghotuls* of this type are found among the Murias near about Kondagaon and Narainpur in Bastar. It is in these *ghotuls* that the unmarried boys and girls gather together during the night.

Some of the *ghotul* houses have also beautiful carvings on the mud walls and the wooden posts. One such Ghotul-guri in Binjoli village about five miles from Narainpur had very fine carvings on two wooden posts, which represent the tribal art as well as the taste for art of these primitive people.

Thus we find that the *ghotul* institution of Bastar is a centre of attraction from a large number of points of views. It is not only the meeting place for the boys and girls of the village, but also has the interest of the elderly people, who also gather there at times of ceremonial occasions and or religious festivities, when the *ghotul* boys and girls entertain them with the music and the dance.

The Machinery of Ghotul

The working of the *ghotul* can be conveniently called the "machinery at work". The Ghotul institution of the Murias is very well organized and exerts its authority over the members of the institution in a number of ways. In Bastar where the Murias have a regular organization, their captain is called Sirdar and the master of the ceremonies, and Kotwar performs the police duty while there are other officials in the *ghotul*, bearing the designation of state officers. The Oraons also have a similar organization and the captain, known as Dhangar Mahato has an acknowledged position among the village officials. "The roots of political organization are to be traced to these dormitories which are characterized by group solidarity and discipline" in the words of D.N. Majumdar.

The secrecy of the institution is guarded strictly; and under no conditions, would a member of the dormitory, be ready to disclose the facts about his institution. "The Dhumkuria fraternity, remarks Dalton, are under the severest penalties bound down to secrecy in regard to all that takes place in their dormitory, and even girls are punished if they dare tells stories." Hutton describing the discipline of the Men dormitories, remarks that "publicity is probably an efficient bar to flirtation". The social solidarity found in the dormitory reflects to a great extent on the tribal life and thus accounts for the spontaneous discipline that characterizes the conduct of primitive life.

The Functionary

The Muria *ghotul* has a hierarchy of functionaries. The names of the officials are often borrowed from the titles of Zamindari or state servants. "The borrowing of official titles and giving the *ghotul* officials these designations after the pattern of the Government or State officials, throw sufficient light on the changed mentality of the Gonds in the words of Indrajit Singh. It is probable that they have been realizing the importance of political institutions and the utility of the various offices therein.

In Padelibhum, the head of the dormitory is always known as the "Leyur Gaita", and below him are the "Leyur Majhi", the "Jalarsi", the "Laharu", the "Baides" and the "Kamdar", as Grigson tells us in his work, *The Maria Gonds of Bastar*

The head officials in the *ghotul* in Narainpur are : Salau, Baidhar, Siladar and Kotwar. Usually a grown up boy, capable of having stranger hold over the members is placed at the head of the *ghotul* organization. He is known as the 'Salau' and is the chief of the *ghotul*, and the supreme head over boys and girls both. He is the captain or the monitor and looks after the general management and upkeep of the *ghotul*. He leads the inmates, 'Cheliks' and 'Motiaris' as the boys and girl members of the *ghotul* are called, when they go out to work or visit other villages with the dance parties and is the final authority in settling disputes among the members of the *ghotul* fraternity. He is also responsible to the elders of the tribe or village for all that happens in the *ghotul*

The Baidhar looks after the collection of fuel, cleaning and sweeping of the *ghotul guree*, the Siladar is responsible for the attendance at the *ghotul*, he has to keep the inmates informed about the programme in the *ghotul* and to report their behaviour to the Salau. The Kotwa does the work of bailiff and has to call the member both male and female, whenever the *ghotul* functions are ordered by the Salau. Besides these there are other officers in rank after the Dewan and the Subedar, and a chain of other minor officers bearing the designation of state officials.

Every official has his respective duties. Similar to these boy-officials, there are the girl-officials also who wield their authority over the girl-circle. They are very much corresponding to the boy-officials their faminine-gender designations being like, the Chalanin; the Tahsildarin, the Kotwarin. They are usually the sweet hearts of the higher officials of the *ghotul*.

The different office-bearers are chosen by the members of the dormitory at a general meeting of the panchayat, which takes place in the *ghotul* premises. It is usually the grown up Cheliks and Motiaris who hold responsible offices of the *ghotul* fraternity. But the head of the *ghotul* is always a man.

Each Chelik (boy) has a Motiari (girl) friend in the *ghotul*, the intimate relation of the pair is continued upto the time till either of the two leaves the *ghotul* on his or her marriage.

The Salau, or the head of the *ghotul*, has certain definite privileges allowed by custom, as, for example, he can have a particular girl as her favourite and declare it in public. The girl of his choice also enjoys certain privileges which may be denied to other girls. The Salau has also the further privilege of having as many girls as he desires to keep with him.

The routine of the *ghotul* is also very interesting. As soon as the girls enter the *ghotul* after supper, they are to bow to the Sirdar or Captain of the dormitory, which is known as the *johare* (salute) after which each girl takes a boy, combs his hair and massages his arms and hands to refresh him. Then they sing and dance together and often tell stories to each other till late at night, when they get tired and retire to their beds.

No doubt, each boy has his girl friend, and the girl her own choice, but the girl takes every care to serve as many boys as she can, and takes care not to arouse the suspicion of other boys or girls of the *ghotul*.

Thus friendship among the pairs of boys and girls and the *ghotul* may grow into intimacies and love which may end into a marriage. The marriages are also probable, since the *ghotul* has members of all the clans of the village, so that the rule of clan-exogamy can also be maintained, while tribal endogamy is already there since all the members of a *ghotul* are essentially members of the Muria community.

A *ghotul* members after marriage is not welcome in the *ghotul*, and they have various methods to keep the married people outside *ghotul*, if so needed by hooks and crooks too.

But where married people are not allowed in the *ghotul*, special consideration is shown to the widows and widowers who want to share the *ghotul*, for there is no restriction against such persons, and they are given as free an entrance as any bachelor member. In the *ghotul* in Narainpur, the Salau or the chief of the *ghotul* was actually a widower, who confidently said of his intentions of never marrying again.

The unions of *ghotul* mates, as well as those between *ghotul* boys and non-*ghotul* girls, or vice-versa are not regarded as complete, unless the married couple after marriage spends a night with the *ghotul* fraternity. It is on this occasion that the *ghotul* ceremonially acknowledges the transfer of loyalty of the newly married couple from the *ghotul* to the village, which henceforth claims their undivided allegiance.

It should also be made clear here, that the love affairs and intimacy within the *ghotul* should in no case be confused with promiscuity or group concubinage. There is definitely a rigid code of honour in the *ghotul*. Decorum is observed and the intimacies of boys and girls though common and usually within the *ghotul* are kept as well guarded secrets from outsiders. Members accused of divulging *ghotul* secrets are severely dealt with and are not permitted to join the dance, neither can they share other activities of the *ghotul* till their fines are fully paid and the offence condoned. This is one of the main reasons why the inmates will withdraw as soon as questions regarding their dormitory life are put to them, and this is why our informants or interviewed persons, kept silent when asked questions by us on this aspect of life during our investigations in Bastar.

"The *ghotul* organisation has a tremendous effect on the social life of the tribes concerned. It is not only a club where the two sexes co-operate in developing tribal solidarity and to direct their energies to productive channels, but it is here, that the necessary training for the duties of tribal manhood is inculcated through a system which has the sanction of tribal experience." Training in discipline is an important feature of *ghotul* organization wherever it exists" – as Majumdar tells us from his own observations. The Muria *ghotul* is more or less independent of tribal control, but the assistance of the *ghotul* can be had by the village on payment of certain specified fee, agreed mutually by the *ghotul* chief and the villagers who are in need of such assistance. In case the headman of the village needs the service of the *ghotul* boys, the chief of the *ghotul* is communicated for help, which, of course, is given ungrudgingly, but individual villagers must pay for their services, which may usually be in the form of same feast or drinks. The wages are usually paid collectively to the Salau or the chief of the *ghotul*, who spends the money on feast and drink in the *ghotul*.

One more important point remains to be emphasized here.

Tribal life in India, as elsewhere, is characterized by an absence of a hierarchy of economic organization. Absence of a well assented division of labour in primitive society does not favour the development of hereditary skill or technique which leads to the formation of artisan classes, or guilds, so that spontaneous co-operation in domestic and economic life becomes essential. The dormitory therefore affords the training ground for educating the children of the village in all matters relating to the social and economic life of the tribes, so that they may participate in all activities of social and economic life. The *ghotul* inmates readily co-operate and extend their help in thatching, erecting cottage and walls, undertaking other house building works, which largely gives them training in these works. During a marriage ceremony in Muria village, the boys and girls jointly get the meals prepared; the boys helping in collecting fuel, etc. and girls cooking the food. The *ghotul* in this way proves a valuable institution for the training and education of the younger generation of the Muria villages in social and economic matters.

Besides this the *ghotul* serves as the centre of training in a number of other matters also. As Majumdar observed in his Presidential Address on "Tribal Culture's Acculturation" in the *Twenty-Sixth Session of the Indian Science Congress*, Lahore in 1939:

> "Lessons in the various agricultural operations, in hunting, in honey-gathering and other minor economic pursuits are imparted in these *ghotuls* through mimetic dances depicting them, while ideas about the sanctity of tribal discipline, social approbation, social justice, reciprocity of obligations, law and

order in society, as well as the relations between efforts and rewards, between crime and punishment, are inculcated through stories and anecdotes which graphically describe individual doings and their repercussions on the social life of the community."

"Besides-this, the ceremonial dancing visits to other *ghotuls* and in some cases to other villages, furnish a background for reciprocity in social obligations."

Over and above all these, sex-training is regarded as an indispensable discipline in dormitory routine, which is regarded as the most vital point in the *ghotul* life. Various methods are adopted to give the inmates a knowledge of sex practices. In the Oraon dormitories, there is a central post, usually the trunk of a tree, in which a slit is made for sexual exercise, and the novice has to mimic sex acts in presence of his elders. In the Muria *ghotul*, the same object is achieved by mimicking sex intercourse by appropriate songs and rhythmic movements of limbs in dances, and through anecdotes describing the method and processes of the sex act, and its importance to tribal life and conduct. Thus the institution serves a greater purpose of training in sex matters.

There are also age-grades in the *ghotul*. The fraternity is divided into groups based on age and although the mean age of the *ghotul* fraternity, as Majumdar tells us, investigated was 14-9, there were as many as 5 grades into which 39 inmates were distributed. Besides these age-grades there were also sex grades and girls were usually kept together unless there were unusual attractions to separate them. The distribution of work by the *ghotul* officials was, as admitted by them, on the basis of this age-grading in the *ghotul*, and every age grade was aware of what its members were expected to do, whenever their services were requisitioned by the village or their labours needed for the *ghotul* itself.

It should also be noted here that the relations of a *ghotul* girl with her family, so long as she remains a member of the *ghotul* are of secondary importance to her, and although she has to do some more routine duties for the family to which she belongs, her interest centres round the life and activities of the institution *ghotul* of which she is a willing participant.

The popularity of a *ghotul* depends upon the personality of *ghotul* boys who can attract girls to the *ghotul*. The popularity is also possible if the girls receive sufficient attention from the boys and also if the *ghotul* programme is more sufficiently attractive for the girls.

Concluding Remark

A very common impression of the *ghotul* that a casual visitor may carry away is that, Muria *ghotul* are nothing but shelters for liaison between young men and women as is the case with the dormitories in Melanesia among the Trobriands. This however, is by no means true of the Muria *ghotul*. The *ghotul*, though giving opportunities of contact between youths, is seldom used us a place for free sexual indulgence. That is positively against the *ghotul* discipline. Among the Murias, we find, it is an institution which seeks to impart education in sex, in agricultural labour and in the art of constructing houses, etc.

In fact, it is used as a preparatory school for young men and women for training in many domestic tasks. Hospitality to guests and entertaining dance parties that visit the village during the dancing season form an indispensable part of the *ghotul* training programme. In addition to the function of tribal schooling, the dormitories are essential limits of the body politic in that they are responsible for supplying labourers in agricultural season, helpful assistants during marriage ceremony and ardent workers during communal feasts and tribal dances. Above all, the dormitory institutions where it exists, ensures tribal endogamy by controlling the movements of women between the tribal area and prohibiting social intercourse between men and women belonging to different tribes."

To sum up the whole issue, the '*ghotul*' is an institution that has manifold uses. It teaches social habits to the youths of both the sexes. It trains them in post-marital behaviour and makes them useful members of society. It inculcates a feeling of tribal discipline, provides a focus for the sentiments of the people, prepares the younger generation to discharge those social and economic obligations without which, collective life of any kind can neither grow nor thrive.

So far as the institution discharges these functions, there is every reason and justification for its survival as such.

11

Mother-Right in India

As is generally agreed upon by most of the writers, ethnologists, and social anthropologists, evolution, may have been in different lines and not necessarily along the same, unilineal one. This view has been associated also with different institutions. Thus with the matriarchal societies there may have been some institutions associated, as it is but logical. Mother-right is an outcome of matriarchal society, usually characterized by matrilineal descent, inheritance, succession and matrilocal residence.

Mother-right Defined

The sociological entity based upon a privileged position of women is differentiated from the complex or complexes of matriarchal culture-circles. "Mother-right" in the sense of this definition thus means, "inheritance in the female line, with regard to relationship as well as to property." as W.H.R. Rivers suggests in his article on 'Mother-right' in the *Encyclopaedia of Religion and Ethics*.

Thus, inheritance from the mother's brother to his nephew is also to be regarded as a matriarchal, though patriarchally influenced, form of inharitance in the female line.

Consequently, it is possible that men become owners, or at least guardians, of a matriarchal joint-family's property, or political rulers in a matriarchal state. His heirs are, in the case of matriarchal survivals, his sister's son, not his own sons, who are regarded as foreign to their father's clan or family. Thus also this form of inheritance will be considered as matriarchal.

Thus we find that 'mother-right' is a phenomena linked with matriarchal societies. Now, matriarchal culture-circles can be regarded, following Grabner and Schmidh and Koppers, as a primary social structure, dependent on the economic role of the women as the first agriculturists. The important position of women can easily be explained as being developed from the originally bilateral social system in the primeval culture.

Those who advocate the precedence of matriarchal over patriarchal forms of society, or matrilineal over a patrilineal mode of descent and inheritance, have sufficient reasoning to lay emphasis on the "mother-right". Since the residence is matrilocal wholly, under matriarchate, and it is the husband who goes to live with his wife in her parent's-house, it is not unusual that he may be often cut as a stranger.

It is also but usual that the woman may have a stronger hold over the family or house in such cases, and she assumes certain amount of authority – which she has not the privilege to enjoy in the societies – where she herself goes to live with her husband (i.e. in patrilocal residence). But we also find that she only is the virtual or formal authority, under matriarchal system, and it is the mother's brother who, in fact, exercises his dominant authority over the family, i.e., his sister's children. But this too will be considered as a form of 'mother-right', for in such cases, whatever authority the maternal uncle, or mother's brother may have. It is only though his sister, or to say on her behalf that he exercises potential authority.

Thus in preference to the father the biological procreator, the mother's brother becomes important for all purposes, and assumes the roles of a sociological father *in toto*. It is the mother's brother who is entrusted with the bringing up of his sister's children, with training them in all the tribal technique crafts and skill, and getting a suitable hand for his nephew or niece when he or she comes of age. It is also not uncommon that he may find such a suitable match for his nephew in her own daughter, under the practice of preferential mating, as is the case with the Todas of South India, the Veddas and in several of the Melanesian tribes. There is also the other possibility of a cross-cousin marriage, such as in which the maternal uncle may marry his son to his sister's daughter. Practically these two forms may coincide through the fact, that the mother's brother by tribal custom usually espouses the father's sister. So far as, this is not the case, marriage of a man with the maternal uncle's daughter is decidedly the more common variety. Thus we find that the mother's brother has a greater role to play in the matriarchal system.

Since, the mother's brother or maternal uncles exercises such a high authority over his sisters' children, it becomes necessary that his nephews and nieces may have some privileges in return. And the nephews are certainly allowed such privileges as may be necessary for keeping the harmonious relation between them. They have a certain degree of privileged familiarity with their maternal uncle, which may be usually in the form of joking-relationship. The nephews are allowed, occasionally to cut jokes with the maternal uncle, and may go even to the extent of cutting jokes relating to their meternal uncle's wife, or the aunt.

Thus whereas, the maternal uncle has an authority over the nephews, the latter are also, in turn given a certain degree of privileged familiarity.

These are only common. Under the avunclulate as the above system is called which itself is associated with a matriarchal system in which the descent and inheritance is traced through the mother, as distinct from the common example of the paternal descent, as in most of our so-called modern communities.

Mother-right thus, we find, has an influence upon it by the factors, such as the matrilineal descent, 'matrilineal succession, matrilineal inheritance of property and laws of matrilocal residence. Mother-right in fact is linked with these, as we have elsewhere maintained.

Looking at the instances of matrilocal residence, we find that a destructive alignment of kin is affected by the matrilineal rule of the many tribes. In the foreign examples, such as those of the Pueblo Indians, mother-right is combined with female ownership of the house. The nucleus of the household consists of the maternal grand-mother, the mother and maternal aunts, the unmarried brothers of the mother, and all the children of the adult women.

The husband of a women lives in his wife's home but without safe tenure of residence rights; in case of divorce, he must leave and will return to the house of his childhood, the one owned by his mother or one of his sisters. This being so, a man continues to live even after marriage to regard his mother's rather than his wife's house as his home. In this way, the children of any family are brought into constant association with their maternal uncles.

Thus we find that the rule of residence may produce a stressing of one side of the family and in so henceforth interfere with the bilateral symmetry of family relations. We also find that under the matrilocal residence, though the father continues to form an economic unit with his wife and her offspring, his authority over the children is at least shared by the men belonging to the house, in which he himself lives as a visitor. The status of the spouse himself is thus profoundly affected. "Obviously, a man occupies a different position under his own roof as regards not only parental but conjugal relations" as Lowie tells us.

In a matrilocal community, he cannot be master of his wife's person in an absolute sense; in any dispute the husband has to reckon with her kin and is liable to be expelled in many cases, if not always. Further, matrilocal residence has a still further effect, as it limits polygyny except in the form of the sororate. A man who goes to live with his wife, does not marry with several wives, except if they happen to be sisters among themselves and are thus living in the same house (matrilocal) where the husband visits them.

The matrilocal residence may also have fluctuating conditions such as under which a husband may very commonly being married live with his parent-in-law; for a part of time going to live with his wife there and fulfilling to all intents and purposes, almost all the functions of a servant, but he sets up an independent household at a later stage, after the birth of children. Each is the practice among the Khasi of Assam. In such cases, it may be conceded that the influence of the maternal kinsfolk is, of course, less pronounced than in permanently matrilocal arrangements.

Thus we see that the matrilocal residence has a greater effect in strengthening the mother-right and making it effective for all purposes. Woman's power under such system is apt to rise higher than under the patriarchal system, where she is rather a stranger.

It has been customary on the part of the older school of anthropologists to regard the matrilineal succession, and matrilineal forms of society preceding the patrilineal, and to seek the "survivals" from a priori matrilineal condition, by which to support their theory; and recently Dr Hartland has again advocated this interpretation with much skill and learning.

Opening the problem of mother-right in his so-named article in *The Making of Man* edited by Calverton, he writes :

> "During many ages the social organization of mankind would not have necessitated the concentration of thought on the problem of paternity. Descent is still reckoned through the mother by a number of savage and barbarous peoples. This mode of reckoning descent is called by useful term of German origin "Mother-right."

It would not be out of place here to refer to the enumeration of the peoples among which mother-right prevails.

In the words of Dr Hartland again, "the civilized nations of Europe and European origin reckon descent and consequently kinship through both parents. A few others, chiefly more civilized nations, like the Chinese and the Arabs, agree with them."

"Apart from these, it may be roughly said that mother-right is found in every quarter of the globe. Not that every people is in the stage of mother-right; on the contrary, many reckon through the father. But even where the latter is the case, vestiges of the former are commonly to be traced."

Hartland would not be content with this much, but would go even further to maintain, that "the result of anthropological investigations during the past half-century has been to show that mother-right everywhere preceded father right, and the reckoning of descent in the modern civilized fashion through both parents."

This is indeed a strange picture of mother-right as drawn by Hartland. But it is useful in as much as it represents the way in which the earlier writers on the mother-right, thought it to be done originated. They thought that mother-right may have been universal in the past historic times, when there was little or no knowledge of paternity, or recognition of father's role in the birth of a child. This ignorance of paternity attached the sole importance to the mother in the birth of child and as a result her position was much accredited. This is found even in many of the native tribes where the lack of knowledge of paternity, grants some privileges to the mother or to her kinds.

> "This past universality of mother-right points to a very early origin. It must have taken its rise in a condition of society ruder than any of which we have cognizance."

In the words of Hartland.

We should also note here that in a society organized by the bond of blood, and where descent is reckoned through females only, the father is not recognized as belonging to the kin of the children. Among the matrilineal peoples exogamy, or marriage outside the kin, is usually, if not always, compulsory.

A corollary of the principle that the father is not a kin to his children is that children of the same father by different mothers are not reckoned as brothers and sisters. This is only a further outcome of the mother-right prevalence, it is pointed out.

Among many of the African peoples, and the Todas of South India, the mother's brother has greater rights over a child than the father, since it is the mother's brother who is the head of the family. So much importance is attached to this person that he is addressed by the same term as father. In many societies, even the duty of blood-revenge falls to him against the father. Wherever progress has been made in the organization of the family, and mother-right is still the basis of organization, as over perhaps the greater part of the African continent, the supreme power is vested in the mother's brother or maternal uncle. In some tribes, as among Loango of Africa he exercises paternal authority over his nephews, whom he can even sell. The father has no power; and if the husband and wife separate, the children follow the mother as belonging to her brother.

They inherit from their mother and not from father; the father's property, after him, passing, to his sister's sons. Thus the inheritance under mother-right, is also in the maternal line. A man cannot pass on his property to his own son, but has to give it to his nephews who are entitled to inherit their maternal uncle's property.

Similarly, the maternal uncle also has to pay the bride-price for the marriage of his sister's son. In turn, he is also liable to receive the bride-price, from the man, who wants to marry his sister's daughter. Thus it is the maternal uncle who has a final voice in the matrimonial set-up also. It is he who fixes or dissolves the marriage.

The husband has thus almost no claims over his children, who are booked after his wife's brother. The mother of the children rather assumes all such claims and can be said to exercise her authority through her brother.

Thus under mother-right, we find that form of relationship between the members of a family also changes. The closest relation is that of mother and child, the next one that of a nephew or niece and uncle or aunt. The uncle owns his nephews and nieces; he can sell them, and they are his heirs, not only in private property, but also in the chieftainship, if he be a chief".

It would be a mistake to consider the uncertainty of paternity alone, as the chief cause of the mother-right. Mother-right is found not merely where paternity is uncertain,but also where it is practically certain. Father-right, on the other hand is found not merely where paternity is certain, but also where it is most uncertain. It follows, therefore, that the uncertainty of paternity cannot be historically the reason for the reckoning of descent exclusively through the mother. There are, besides other reasons too, which cause such a system.

In India, mother-right can be traced along two or three lines as Ehrenfels has treated the problem in his work *Mother-right in India*. They are:-

(i) Single cultural elements of matriarchal character: Those characteristic of sociology, religion or ergology which can historico-athnolopogically be proved to have been peculiar to matriarchal culture - areas, and to have spread exclusively within their sphere of influence, are classed under this heading.

(ii) Social elements: Inheritance of property and descent in the female line, prominent position of the mother's brother in social or religious life, polyandry, permission of divorce in monandric marriages, sexual freedom of girls before marriage, or comparatively insignificant punishments, which can be recognized as only recently introduced, for sexual intercourse with caste members, puberty rites of girls, a special form of cross-cousin marriage, forcing, or at least making it desirable for a boy to marry the daughter of his mother's brother, the couvade etc.

(iii) Religious elements: Goddesses or female ancestors, creating the particular caste or tribe as social unit, ancestor-worship, generally, female temple servants - (Devdasis), priestesses or dancing girls, rain-fecundily, charms perhaps double trials, and all the different mythological figures, customs and rites in so far as they clearly exhibit matriarchal traces.

Besides this wide list, Ehrenfels, notes certain other elements, which he considers as "matriarchal survivals".

Among them, the following are prominent, according to him; remarriage of widows and divorced women (where it is practised), contain forms of levirate wedding, economic independence of women and girls' education on similar lines with boys' education are cultural features which, in India, must be considered as matriarchal survivals, "unless they date back to Islamic, Hebrew, Christian or Zorastrain influences. Worship of the goddess of contagious diseases and certain forms of animal sacrifice, where decapitation is prominent, the importance of blood or the colour red in religious, observances to a certain extent, perhaps also the Megalithic cultural elements, may be thus classified in Ehrenfels view. On the other hand hatchet agriculture cannot be considered as pointing to matriarchal influence on Indian soil, which has been tilled for at least five millenniums.

Among the communities in India, where the mother-right has its wide sway, we can mention the Khasis of Assam speaking Austro-Asiatic languages the Garo-living in the neighbourhood of the Khasis, the Kadirs of Cochin and Coimbatore district, the Todas of the Nilgiri Hills and the Nayars of South India.

A brief description of these, and of some of their specific "mother-right" features would not be out of place here, for an illustration.

The Khasis of Assam

The Khasis are the most important representatives of the North-East group of Indian mother-right observers, "combining a sense of "independence" and activity with a conservative adherence to their relatively old form of mother-right; so characteristic of these hillmen", in the words of Ehrenfels.

The Khasis as a higher unit comprise several minor groups or tribes. Each of these tribes is divided into two to six principally endogamous sub-groups which are composed of exogamous units on clans, as Gordan puts it, all clansmen tracing their descent to one and the same female ancestor who is called the mother of the root. The husbands matrilocally live in their wives' households, or reside at their mothers' houses. Private property is inherited according to the conception, daughters being their mother's heirs, the youngest sister getting the lion's share in the shape of the family house, its main pieces of furniture and the mother's jewellry. "Neither sons, nor brothers inherit". The descent is also in the female line. The Khasi religion also shows markedly matriarchal traces. The creative force is usually a female deity. The high priestess is a woman.

The Kadirs of Cochin

Among the Kadirs of Cochin, most of the occupation are carried by the women. The economic activity of men seems to be restricted to hunting and collecting forest produce. Marriage of boys with paternal relatives is banned, and the marriage of a boy to his maternal uncle's daughter is preferred. The remarriage of widows is prohibited. There is lack of direct succession in the female line. This lack of direct succession in the female line is perhaps only due to the poverty in private property of the Kadir ergology and also to the lack of any social organization, other than small, nomadic village units.

The Todas

The Todas, who are one of the important peoples of South Indian tribes, inhabit the Nilgiri hills, and the Malabar. The Todas have some social characteristics which seem to prove them related even to the most advanced caste, i.e., the Nayars of the South-Western mother-right group, as e.g., ritual defloration which was formerly connected with puberty rites, or the custom of polyandry.

The Todas at any rate, must be considered as belonging to the primitive tribes of the mountains in the South-Western area of Indian mother-right without being part and parcel of the savage jungle-tribe type of that region. The Todas practice polyandry.

The Nayars

The Nayars of the Travancore Cochin are the characteristic type of mother-right observers. The Nayars are the polyandrous people.

The married women do not sleep in the common dormitory; she has one or two rooms of her own, where she can receive her husband, or in former days, her husbands. The fathers showed relatively little interest in the education of their children, a feature not common in other mother-right people, which might perhaps really be considered an outcome of the Nayar's military occupation.

As Logan has observed: "The Nayar women are as chaste and faithful as their neighbours, just as they are modest."

The maternal uncle plays an important part, not only as the 'Kasaravaṇ', the representative of the formerly ruling mother, but also in many other respects. The maternal uncle's song the "Amma Champattu" as it is called is sung at marriage. Children to a certain degree belong to their mother's brother, whose name occurs in theirs". The eldest daughter of the eldest mother in a house, is of great importance, and formerly ruled as a "prime-minister" of her mother. Her brothers too obeyed to orders. Thus we understand that the family was dearer to a Nayar than anything else in the world.

The Nayars represent the typical mother-right system as we can say.

Summing up the whole of the case, we can maintain that mother-right is a characteristic phenomena of the matrilineal societies which reflects mother's (women's) authority in the family or the household in those societies where her social status is esteemed rather high and her importance is well realized.

12

Caste System in India: A Critical Appraisal in Historical and Functional Perspectives

A PROBLEM Much Concerned with social stratification, is that of caste-system. Caste system is a unique institution in India, and also an institution unique to India. The word 'caste' comes from the Portuguese word - 'casta' - meaning 'breed' or 'race'.

The caste system has been studied mostly from the academic points of view, and much of the literature on the subject refers to the origin and history of the institution on its evil consequences. As Hutton remarks in his basic work *Caste in India*, "It is no doubt the manifold origin of caste in India that is the cause of its being unique, since it is unlikely that a complex combination of factors could be exactly repeated in some other part of the world."

Now before proceeding to discover the origins of the caste-system, i.e., how such a unique institution came to exist in India, and before proceeding still further, to ascertain the functions it fulfils, let us first of all, see what the caste is, and how has it been defined by various writers.

What is Caste?

Risley, who was probably the first ethnographer to deal with the problem in India, defines the caste "as a collection of families or groups of families having a common name from a mythical ancestor, mythological or divine, professing to follow some hereditory occupation and regarded as forming single homogeneous community."

Katkar, an Indian writer on the caste-system, defines caste "as a social group, having two characteristics:

(i) membership being confined to those who are born of the caste-members, and including all persons so born.
(ii) these members being forbidden by the social laws to marry outside the caste group..

But this definition cannot be said to be applicable in all cases, in some castes members may be recruited from outside (other castes) also, as we find in the case of Humbalwari caste of Central Malabar.

N.K. Dutta, another distinguished writer on the subject, in fact, abstains from laying down any definition of the caste, and only describes some of the features of caste. According to him, a caste is characterized by the following features :

(i) members of a caste cannot marry outside the caste-group. There are also similar, though less rigid restrictions on eating and drinking with members of another caste. This restriction on inter-dining is called 'non-commonsalic'.
(ii) There are fixed occupations for fixed castes, i.e. every caste has its own occupation, which it follows.
(iii) There are also some sort of hierarchical gradations in the caste-system, with a high gradation at the top as the Brahmana-system in case of the Hindu-caste-system.
(iv) Birth determines a child's caste, or to say a man inherits his caste from the very birth. Unless he be expelled from the caste for violation of its rules or he unless deliberately leaves a caste, and joins another, transition from one caste to another is not possible.

This description seems a satisfactory one to some extent, since it lays down some specific features, which give us some understanding of the caste-system, which is otherwise essentially such a Hindu state that it is difficult to understand.

A recent writer on castes, Ghurye has emphasized the great role played by the Brahmin priestly caste in India. According to him, caste is "a Brahmanic child of the Indo-Aryan culture cradled in the land of the Ganges" and thence transferred to other parts of India by the Brahmin prospectors. He also thinks that endogamy, the outstanding feature of the system was first developed by the Brahmins in the plains of northern India and thence conveyed as a culture-trait to the other areas.

We find that there are in India various types of endogamy, tribal, geographical, territorial, sectarian and even linguistic. All these can hardly be accounted for by diffusion. The "mana" concept, for example, suggests Dr Majumdar, could produce tribal endogamy in India and regional boundaries have affected marriage field in several parts of India. Caste-principles are often found functioning in areas remote from Brahmanic influence which has provided material on the basis of which Hutton has worked out his pre-Aryan theory of caste, which we shall discuss later on in the present essay.

Hutton's View of Caste

Thus agreeing with Hutton we can say that each caste is a social unit in itself. The customs by which it lives are generally different in some respects from those of other castes. As noted above, persons of one caste do not marry those of another. The extent to which persons of one caste will eat or drink with those of another is strictly limited by written laws and everybody knows who is affected by them. Even a change of religions may not destroy the caste-system, for Muslims, who do not recognize it as valid, are often found to observe it in practice, and there are many Muslims castes and when some reforming body breaks away from Hinduism and repudiates caste, it becomes something very like a new caste of its own.

There are some three thousand castes in India, and as Hutton says, it would need an encyclopaedia to deal with them all.

The Origin of the Caste-system

The subject of the origin of the caste-system is a complicated affair. No point has been so controversial in Indian ethnology, as perhaps, the problem of the origin of caste-system, and two writers have ever agreed upon the suggestion for the origin. Each writer on caste-system seeks to explain the origin of the caste in his own way.

Thus various theories have been put forward to account of the origin of caste in India. The important among them is what is called the Traditional theory of caste, which is, in fact, derived from, or based upon the accounts given in the Vedas etc.

As Dr Majumdar suggests, the complex nature of caste structure is evident from the fact that after a century of painstaking and meticulous research in the history and function of the social system, we do not possess yet a valid explanation of the circumstances that might have contributed to the formation and development of this unique system. "There are today as many theories of the caste origins as the number of those who have written on it. Yet it must be admitted that no social institution except totemism has been studied from so varied angles as the caste-system of India.

The Traditional Theory

The traditional theory of caste explains the origin of caste in India through the four Varnas, the Brahmin, Kshatriya, Vaishya and Shudra, and origin of all other castes and sub-castes from "hypergamy" between these four principle castes, the accounts of which are contained in the Vedas.

The ancients who believed in the divine descent of man and in special creation have explained the caste system as derived from the person of the Supreme Creator, Brahma. This theory has been described by the Hindu law-giver Manu with a wealth of details, which is still accepted by the orthodox section of the population in India. So long as religion will keep its hold on the minds of people, this theory must appeal to many. The orthodox theory can be divided into two parts. While the first is theoretical in the sense that it assumes a mystical origin of the four Varnas, the second explains the working of the four-fold social division and is partly historical and partly functional. The fact that many of the castes are hybrid ones which have resulted from inter-marriage on the principles of hypergamy and of *anuloma* or prescribed, and *pratiloma* or forbidden unions, as they are found even in the present times, has given some status to the orthodox point of view. If however, the divine origin of the Varnas is an allegorical explanation of the functional division of society, the theory assumes practical significance in the opinion of Dr. Majumdar.

This traditional theory had a profound influence on the early thoughts in India which sought to explain the origin of the caste system as such and even to this day is not wholly neglected by the author.

Nesfield's Theory of Occupational Basis

Another theory advanced to suggest the origin of caste-system is that by Nesfield who attempted to explain it on the basis of occupations. The association of castes with occupations has suggested functional interpretation of the social system, and some writers have gone so far as to claim that "function and function alone is responsible for the origin of the caste-system". 'The social distance between castes, high and low, arises according to them, from the nature of the occupations, the superiority or inferiority of the caste being determined by the superiority or inferiority of the occupation followed by the caste. This hypothesis, we find, ignores the racial point of view, for as Nesfield holds, there is "No" social difference between castes, the only difference being in the function followed by the people.

But, as Dr Majumdar remarks:

> "There may not be such racial difference between the higher castes as such, there may not be great variation of physical features in groups occupying a particular geographical region or parts of it, but some racial difference between 'high' and 'low' social groups does exist and is apparent to one who knows the country and its people. We also note that even if there does not exist any ethnic dissimilarity between the castes, the few occupations followed in India do not account for the innumerable castes that one finds in any particular region. That makes the functional interpretation of the Hindu social system, extremely dubious, though function is one of the main planks on which the social stratification is obviously based, or had its moorings in the past."

Nesfield regards caste to be based on occupational basis, and emphasizes this fact by remarking that the artisans rank higher than the basket-makers in the Indian caste-system. He regards caste, "as a natural product of society in the creation of which, religion played no part at all". He has elaborated this view in his essay, 'Brief View of the Caste-system'.

This theory, though suggests an important factor to be at work in the origin of the caste-system, i.e. that of occupation, is criticised on a number of grounds :

(i) Firstly we find that agriculturists come from all castes, and not from any particular caste, in India. This shows that occupation is no hard and fast rule for the caste distributions. Members of different castes may follow the same occupation, as we find in practice too.
(ii) In India, we find three thousand castes but not three thousand occupations corresponding to these castes.

Chanda's View

Chanda traces caste to 'race function'. According to him, colour or race-differences real and fancied together with hereditary functions gave birth to caste-system, but as newer groups formed or attached themselves to the Aryan nation, the absurdity of repudiating them all as distinctly coloured or 'Varnas' was recognized and the theory of *Varnashankar* or mixed caste was started to explain their origin.

Thus, these writers from India, who have studied the native Hindu-caste system, suggest origin in their own ways.

The Racial Theory of Risley

The racial significance of the caste-system was first recognized by Sir Herbert Risley. Risley traced the origin of castes from the Indo-Aryan immigration into India.

He maintains in in his book, *The People of India* that "Race and hypergamy are responsible for caste system". Thus social differences were recognised similarly due to colour differences, and this gave rise to a system of hypergamy. In order to base caste on hypergamy, Risley finds it necessary to pre-suppose a hypothetical point at which the result of inter-marriage between the fair invaders and the dark aborigines provides enough women for the society in question to close its ranks and become a caste, although there still exist outside it more women of the same community from which it has been drawing its wives and with which it has been in more or less intimate relations. The prehistoric migrations of the Indo-Aryans from Persia, where a four-fold division of society was known, laid down the structure of social grouping in his view. "The clash and fusion of cultures between the invading people, on the one hand and the indigenous on the other who belonged to separate racial stock inferior to immigrants, brought about the super-structure, which is the caste-system. Endogamy which is a fundamental trait of the caste-system was absent in Persia. The racial dissimilarity between the invaders and the invaded emphasized the importance of the breed, while cultural differences between them did not encourage amalgamation or large-scale miscegenation." A compromise was worked out, inter-marriage was allowed till such time as it was necessary. In other words, a *jus connubii* was formed, after which the various invading-groups closed their ranks to the indigenes. That is how, Hindu-law-giver recognized inter-marriage as it was felt necessary. It is still practised in the act-lying parts, for example, among the Rajputs and Brahmins of the Cis-Himalayan-region.

The position of Negroes in the Southern states of U.S.A. has been cited as a parallel case and the view is supported by Westermarck. But this theory does not explain the pollution which may take place, when members to the two castes meet and come into contact with each other. This theory can explain the endogamous character of the caste and the caste solidarity to a large extent.

N.K. Dutta, while criticising Risley, adopts his racial theory of origin in effect, though he attaches more value than Risley to the account of caste in the code of Manu.

Dr Ghurye, who worked extensively with the problem of caste-system in India, regards caste as having arisen largely as a result of racial differences. Ghurye also emphasizes, particularly the factor of priestly manipulation by Brahmans, attempting to maintain the purity of racial invaders. We may remark here, that one cannot but believe, however, that for priestly interference of this kind to be effective in setting up so far-reaching and complicated a system as that of caste, it is necessary to assume the pre-existence of certain of the essential factors in that system which would predispose the population generally to accept an extension of them. Colour prejudice and racial exclusiveness have been common enough in the racial history of the world, but they have nowhere else led to such an institution as caste. Thus it would be rash to suppose that they could have done so in India of themselves. On the other hand, race and colour prejudice, have no doubt made an important contribution to the development of the caste-system, and it may be that they have played such a part in the crystallizing of that institution as to justify the statement that not have come down to posterity in its subsequent generations, having been the subject to the reagent of the racial prejudice and discrimination.

The Guild Theory of Ibbetson

An important theory to suggest the origin of caste-system in India is what is called the Guild theory put forward by Ibbetson.

Ibbetson has, like Ghurye, laid great emphasis on the exploitation of their position by the Brahman caste which he supposes to have "degraded all occupations except their own and that of their patrons of the ruling class." He explains caste as arising from a combination of tribal origins, functional guilds and a 'Lenitical religion', and has laid the greater stress on the tribe. It is, of course, clear enough that certain tribes are responsible for the formation of certain castes, and no less clear that certain castes are, or have been in the past, restricted to certain occupations, but Ibbetson's explanation of the origin of caste is really only a summary of certain of its obvious features. "These features of tribes, guilds and religious monopolies have no doubt constituted to the growth and extension of the caste-system, and done much to consolidate and perpetuate it, but they cannot be regarded as causes. They are features which are not unique but common to many societies in many countries, but did not produce a system like that of the caste, as it is found in India. As Hutton suggests here, "Given caste, a tribe, a guild, or a priestly order may very easily becomes a caste, but failing the essentials of the caste-system, there is nothing in them, with the possible exception of the priestly order, which will produce a caste."

The Ritualistic Explanation of Hocart

Quite a different origin for caste is argued by Hocart, who apparently regards the whole system as originating in ritual. His theory is known as the 'ritualistic' explanation of caste, as it seeks to discover the origins of caste in the ancient rituals. He regards the four Varnas as a division of the people devised primarily for ritualistic purposes; they represent the four points of the compass, as do the colours, white, red, yellow and black. The ritual appears to be a duplication of some ancient fertility rite in which two divisions of the people were involved, representing the sky and the earth, and to be focussed on the king as representing the deity, or being himself the deity incorporate, and the functions of various 'castes' are derived from the offices performed by them in the daily ritual of the royal court, Hocart's conclusions are, however, based on his observation of the existing ritual of the Buddhist Temple of the Tooth at Kandy, and not on direct acquaintance with caste in India.

Slater's Theory

A theory of the origin of caste, which combines both functional and racial origins has been put forward by Slater, in his work *Dravidian Elements in Indian Culture*. He emphasizes the fact that caste arose in India, before the Aryan invasion as a result of occupations becoming hereditary and marriage being arranged by parents within the society of the common craft because sexual maturity was early and trade secrets were preserved.

As a result of magic and religious ceremonies also, exclusive occupational groups were built up, marriage outside which became prejudicial and contrary to practice. The Aryan invasion had the effect of strengthening a tendency to associate difference of caste with a difference of colour, and also of strengthening a tendency for castes to be placed in a scale of social precedence.

Some Other Views with Regard to Origin of Caste

Dutta takes a somewhat similar view of the impact of an Aryan culture upon pre-Aryan occupational classes already endogamous on account of occupational prejudice and the preservation of trade secrets.

Olderburg regards caste as derived from class, guild and tribe, segregated into permanently separate groups by heredity and by restrictions on marriage and commensality and fear of pollution, which were derived partly from the Aryan invader and partly from the aboriginal inhabitants.

This fear of pollution has also been stressed by Ketkar, who points out that "the chief principle on which the entire system depends is that of purity and pollution" - a view which has not escaped Ghurye and which has been also endorsed by Sarat Chandra Ray.

Linton has drawn attention to the probability that India, or some part of India, formed at some time in its past, part of the ostronician religion, in which has been since Palaelithic times a fundamental pattern of organization on the basis of small endogamous groups.

This pattern, he says, assumes various forms, but it is linked up with a predominant importance of kinship as a basis for organising the reciprocal behaviour of the group members. In such a system, he suggests, it would lead to frequent invasions and to the emergence of an urban culture, and to developing guild systems to their logical conclusions.

S.C. Roy's View in Mana Origin

These theories of origin, so far referred, contain some important contribution, but scarcely any of them lays enough emphasis on the importance of primitive conception of taboo, 'mana', and soul-stuff, contributing to its function. This cannot justly perhaps be said of Sarat Chandra Roy, who does indeed accept the hypothesis that a belief in 'mana' and 'soul-substance' has contributed to the development of caste, which he regards as "the outcome of the interaction between the Indo-Aryan 'Varna' system on the one hand and the tribal-system of the pre-Dravidian and the occupational class system of the Dravidian, on the other." These he regards as having been cemented into the caste-system by the Indo-Aryan concept of 'Karma' and a certain "taboo-holiness" that came to be attached to the Brahmana for his accredited possession of a special spiritual energy (*brahma-sakti*) born out of the predominance of the 'Sativa guna' (fundamental quality of revealing light) sustained and stabilized through well-disciplined continuance.

The emphasis laid on the contribution of the 'Karma' concept is important, but generally speaking Roy seems to attach too much weight to the philosophic aspects of Hinduism and attempts to interpret the institution of caste in terms of ethical principles and an idealism which probably had little to do with its primary origin.

Thus we find a number of theories have been advanced by the different authors to account for the origin of caste, and each explains it in its own way.

Conclusion

Concluding this discussion of the origin of the caste system, it can be said, on the basis of our study of the subject, as above, that the following factors may have contributed to the emergence of the caste-system:

(i) The geographical isolation of the Indian peninsula as a whole, and the individual areas within it, may have largely facilitated the origin and growth of such a unique institution as the caste-system in India.

(ii) The primitive ideas of the (belief in) power of food to transmit qualities must also have been a major factor in the development of this institution. For a possible source of the commensal taboo, however, we need not look far from that of the occupational one.

(iii) Similar ideas of totemism, taboo, mana, and 'soul-stuff' – all may have worked towards the direction of the growth of caste-system.
These beliefs in life-matter, or soul-stuff, are closely associated with belief in 'mana' and with the practice of magic.

(iv) Ideas of pollution, ablution, purification and ceremonial purity with associations of ritual sacrifice.

(v) Ideas of the exclusive family, ancestor worship and the sacramental meal.

(vi) Beliefs in 're-incarnation' and in the doctrine in 'Karma'.

(vii) Beliefs in magic associated with crafts and functions.

(viii) Hereditary occupations, and trade and craft secrets.

(ix) Guilds and associations of that character and various factors in the development of economic life.
(x) Clash of antagonistic cultures, particularly between cultures with matrilineal and 'patrilineal modes of descent.
(xi) Clash of races, colour prejudice, and conquest.
(xii) The development of classes with exclusive religious and social privileges.
(xiii) Individual isolation of tribes and polities, and their inclusion without absorption in larger administrative units.
(xiv) Deliberate economic and administrative policies.
(xv) Exploitation by a highly intelligent but by no means, 'entirely altruistic hierarchy which had evolved a religious philosophy too subtle for the mass of the people.

To sum up, it can be said a number of factors, even too far to visualize, and too remote to appear as relevant factors at present, may alone have been combined with other more potential causes to give birth, and later to the growth of such a unique, yet so well-established an institution as the caste system of India.

Caste Functions

The caste-system in India, which is a unique institution on the Indian soil, exists largely because of the functions which it discharges and is useful thus in the Indian culture. It would be worthwhile here, to discuss the functions of the caste in India.

From the Individual's Point of View

First of all, from the point of view of the individual members of a caste, the system provides him from birth with a fixed 'social mileu' from which neither wealth nor poverty success nor disaster, can remove him, unless of course he so violates the standards of behaviour laid down by his caste that spews him forth – temporarily or permanently.

1. He is provided in this way with a permanent body of association which controls almost all his behaviour and contacts. It

is the caste which determines scope of his marriage, i.e., where he can marry, what trades or professions he can carry and so on. Thus the practice of his caste also, dictates to each member customs to be observed in the matter of diet, the observance of ceremonial uncleanliness, and whether he may, or may not, marry or remarry widow.

2. We find, thus that "with regard to the individual, the function of caste is to predetermine his 'pattern of behaviour' in this world to a very considerable degree of nicety, leaving much less to individual choice, than is usual in a casteless society" - as Dr. Huttan suggests.

Thus from the point of view of the individual himself, the caste-system is a great help and guide in his life.

From the Point of View of the Community

1. From the aspect of the caste community itself caste determines the membership of the community. This may sound like strange, but a little effort in understanding it would make the case clear enough. It is true that in the case of some castes, particularly those of sectarian origin, recruitment from outside may be possible, but generally speaking, a caste cannot increase the membership of its body except by means of an increase in the number of births within the caste.

2. Caste again determines to a very large extent the social status of each caste in regard to other castes.

3. Further, the caste system enables to act corporately and to control the behaviour of its component members. It is able in this way to raise its position in society. As Hutton suggests, by organization and propaganda, a caste can even change its name in the course of time, get a new one accepted, and by altering its canons of behaviour in the matter of diet and marriage, increase the estimation in which it is held.

Caste then may in some cases serve communities but never individuals, as a ladder for rising in the social scale.

It is no doubt one of the functions of a social system to hand on from generation to generation that pattern of skill, knowledge and behaviour which we speak of as culture, the benefits and advances achieved in man's struggle to control environment, using that word in its widest sense, of course. Caste secrets are well safeguarded and perpetuated by occupational castes, and the castes generally functions as a guild or a trade union.

In the religious sphere, the caste system so operates that the caste can change or modify its social and religious observances in accordance with changing 'ethical standards' or the trend of public opinion.

The third aspect of the functions of caste, and the most important is that which has regard to the State and to the society as a whole. The functions which caste performs for the individual may be and are performed for individuals by other institutions in other societies.

Turnivall in his *Netherlands India* has described British India as the outstanding instance of a country, whom he calls *a plural society*, has proved stable.

Other Important Functions

Let us now examine in brief some other important functions of castes:

(i) It will be understood from our study of the caste system, that are important function of caste, perhaps the most important of all its functions, and the one which above all others makes caste in India, "a unique institution", is, or has been to integrate Indian society, to weld into one community the various competing if not incompatible groups composing it.

(ii) A second very important function of caste has been to act as a political stabilizer. It was this function, apparently of the caste system which so moved the administration of the Abbe' Dubois, who considered the caste system of the Hindus, "the happiest effort" of their legislation. He regarded the caste system as being responsible for the preservation of India from complete barbarism, and as the sure basis of orderly government, as a defence against despotism, and as a means of preserving the arts, and as a means of preserving the Hindu pattern of culture under the regime of alien culture.

(iii) Again, the caste system does provide for the various functions necessary to social life, functions ranging from education to scavenging, from government to domestic service of the most menial kind.

(iv) Indeed as Blunt insists that the caste system is so mutable that no account of it remains for long; "its evolution is still proceeding: new castes and sub-castes came into existence, old customs fall into abeyance"

This, no doubt, is true enough, but it is not the system that is changing so much as caste details within it. Caste, no doubt, keep changing and customs come and go; the pattern alters, but the principles that govern it, the frame that holds the pattern, so to speak, are exceptionally constant for a human institution.

An Indian writer, Pramath Nath Bose, in his work, *History of Hindu Civilization during British rule*, has stated that "the caste has acted essentially to impose that attitude of mind needed to raise men from savagery but to stop them half way on the road to progress".

"Caste makes no compromises", says Sherring. "The most ignorant Hindu is able to compel the obedience of the most intelligent".

We may note here one point and that is, that it is a possible further disadvantage of the caste system economically, that it probably discourages organization from above by the 'entrepreneur' no less than it forestalls combination on the part of the workman.

The Hindu caste system, as also others, we find, has 'a specific religious relation'. It has been held to be have been established by divine ordinance or at least with divine approval and the Bhagwada Gita, which probably more nearly than any other sacred 'scripture' fulfils metaphysical needs of the Hindus, the function performed by the Quaran or for Christians by the Bible, contains some well-known lines which inculcate the supreme merit of performing one's caste duties. "One's own duty (i.e. *dharma* or caste rules), though defective, is better than another's duty well performed. This is the conjunction of the great epic.

Some Main Drawbacks

Thus we have seen that the caste system has a number of functions and that it serves as most important basic institution to keep the group or community solidarity intact. Yet even so important an institution too is not totally devoid of vitiations some of which become quite apparent in course of time and have been subjected to severe criticism.

First and foremost is that the caste-system as it exists in India today, creates the outcaste and high-caste feeling which results in an unending antogamism between the two. This also results in the inferiority and superiority-feeling in men, the former causing an obstacle in the free development of an individual's personality. The majority of the Indian population has suffered much due to this ill out-caste-feeling, as a result of which great reformatory-movement were being carried by the nationalist leaders of India and much has been done by the national government also, since the time of its coming into power, in the direction of controlling 'out-casteiasm' as we may call it.

It seems the Hindu Code Bill would be a permanent guarantee against this ill-doctrine of out-casteisms.

Another major drawback of the caste-system is the hardship which is entailed on generations of women in all those castes that aim at raising their position on the social scale. "Any caste, or subcaste that wishes to rise in the estimation of its fellows, or to claim an origin from some twice-born *varna* to which it is not generally conceded to belong, finds it essential to confirm as nearly as may be the 'traditional standard of Brahmana castes in the matter of insisting on the marriage of girls before they reach the age of puberty, and in forbiddening their remarriage, even if widowed in infancy.

The miserable condition of the outcastes is reflected in the *Censuses of India*. The number of these 'exterior castes' in India was found at the Census of 1931 to be more than 50 millions, or 21% on a Hindu population of 239 odd millions. It is quite clear that the unfortunate position of exterior caste could be remedied without destroying the caste system. Their position is the result of prejudice and taboos which have been operative during millennia, and cannot be got rid of in a night. That is a process which can be accomplished in the course of time with gradual reformation, and with the help of education, in its broadest sense. To destroy the caste system, even if it could be done, might be disastrous to the society which is constructed on its framework. Religious beliefs make it tolerable, and even reasonable to members of that society, as Hutton suggests.

Looking at the problem of caste in the reviewing perspective, we find, that 'caste is probably what Professor Bartlett, would call one of the *Land Joints* of Hindu culture, and any attempt to modify by a direct attack on it, is likely to provoke resistance and discord, and reformers will need to aim at some 'soft point' some other feature of the culture, that is, through which the 'hard point' can ultimately be circumstance and isolated. The mere fact that caste is one of the chief differentiating cultural features between western cultures and Hinduism, is, if Professor Bartlett is to be followed, a reason for scrupulously avoiding direct attack on it.

As Hutton has suggested, there is yet another function which the caste-system probably performs, and that is a genetic one. India is a country in which the male sex generally outnumber the female. Thus it is possible, according to Hutton that the caste-system itself contributes to the preponderance of masculinity. Westermark's *History of Human Marriage* takes the view that a mixture of race leads to an increase in the ratio of females to males. The endogamy prevents external hybridize while the internal exogamy prevents the possibility of a fresh pure line, arising within the old one, by the isolation of any character not common to the whole line.

Caste, therefore, would appear to be of definite assistance to the Hindu in his superlative anxiety for male offspring.

Summing up the whole case, and weighing the arguments advanced for and against the caste-system, we can say that "caste is a dynamic system and the oft-repeated rebuke by foreign writers, that caste is not incompatible with nationalism, is based on prejudice, if not ignorance. Agreeing with Majumdar, we can remark, that fusion as well as fission, are the principles of evolution, just as the multiplication and division of the cells, and cultural dynamics can forge solidarity, if that is essential for survival. Caste would continue to have sufficient reasoning for its existence so far this holds true, and would largely have a survival value - as such.

13

The Scope of Social Anthropology and Applied Anthropology

ANTHROPOLOGY, the science of man, has extended its range of application to such an extent today that it has developed a new branch, called Applied Anthropology which concerns with the application of the principles of the anthropological science to practical fields. There are now few of major human problems left to which the science of man cannot suggest an adequate solution.

This indigent extension of anthropological knowledge in the practical field has been growing more in the last one or two decades. The purpose of the present essay is only to ascertain and examine the scope of anthropology.

The subject of the "scope of applied anthropology" can be very well discussed in replying to this sort of question "What is the purpose of studying anthropology?"

As Evans-Pritchard has shown, while discussing the problem of applied anthropology that this question can be variously interpreted and answered. It can be interpreted as an enquiry about the motives that govern a man to take up social anthropology as a profession. Anthropologists would differ among themselves in giving answers to this question. Some would even say that 'they don't quite know', or in the tone of some enthusiastic American scholars, "I guess, I just like going to places. But this does not actually satisfy our curiosity for the scope of anthropology.

The question raised above about the purpose of the study of anthropology has generally the sense of – "What is the use of the knowledge about primitive society?" This can be further subdivided into two forms:

(i) What is the use of such study to the primitive people? and

(ii) What is the value to men who study it i.e. the anthropologists?

As we well know that the social anthropologists mostly study primitive societies, and, therefore, the information they collect and the conclusions to which they come from there, have necessarily some bearings on the problems of the administration and education of the primitive peoples. And if the knowledge about primitive society can be utilised by a government or by those entrusted with the task for the benefit or betterment of the natives, the very foundations of the scope of applied anthropology are laid here. It can be reasonably acknowledged that if the policy of the government aims to govern the natives through their chiefs, it becomes not only useful, but also essential to know who are the chiefs and what are their functions and authority, privileges and obligations in their own society. In the same way, if a government intends to govern a people according to their own laws and customs, it becomes necessary to discover those laws and customs. So also is true in the case of economy.

If it is intended to change a people's economy, for example, to alter their system of land tenure, or to encourage them to grow export crops, or to institute markets and money economy, it is of some advantage to be able to estimate at any rate roughly – what social effects these changes are likely to bring about. This was realised early both by the government and the anthropologists.

The missionaries had also realised that in order to convert a native people to Christianity, some knowledge of their own religious beliefs and practices is required. All these objectives gave impulse to the value of the study of anthropology and in the meanwhile led to the anthropological knowledge in the practical field.

This value of applied anthropology to administration was recognized earlier in England. At that time England was the biggest colonial power which the colonies almost all over the world in South Africa, India, Burma, Malaya, Ceylon, and in the far East countries. From the beginning of the present century, both the colonial office and the colonial governments, have shown an increasing interest in anthropological teaching and research. Thus the provision was made by them for the colonial cadets to undertake among other courses of instruction, instruction in social anthropology at Oxford and Cambridge, and more recently in London.

The colonial officers were also brought home for refresher courses at these three universities, since the last was highly accredited and some of them chose social anthropology, as an optional subject. In addition to these, administrative officers have often taken the Anthropological Tripos at Cambridge and occasionally the Diploma or a Post-graduate course at Oxford, and a great many among them have kept in touch with anthropological developments through membership of the Royal Anthropological Institute. Anthropologists are included in various advisory committees of the colonial office and also on the committees for the development of colonial studies at various British Universities. Applied Anthropology with reference to the colonial problem is taught at the London School of Economics and Political Science, the London School of Education and at several other places, and the Royal Anthropological Institute has a special committee on the subject.

"It has become axiomatic in colonial regions that wise and efficient administration must be based on careful study of local conditions and sympathetic understanding of the social peoples" – as Telix M. Keesing has remarked in *The Science of Man in the World Crises*, edited by Ralph Linton.

Hence administrators, traders and also missionaries, have turned increasingly to the science for information and guidance. Just as they have looked to geology, entomology and the other physical and biological sciences in handling resources of territories concerned, and to tropical medicine in meeting health problems, so they have drawn upon anthropology to throw light on the exceedingly difficult problems of human relations, especially to the adjustment of the so-called "native" or indigenous populations to modern civilization. This is only for the obvious reason that those who are in the major charge of administrators and others concerned with colonial welfare have also been the focus for the anthropological study. Thus we find that by whether by way of professional workers or otherwise, applied anthropology, i.e., "the use of the view point, knowledge and techniques of the science as an aid in solving the practical problems" – has been most fully developed and tested along the colonial frontiers of the world.

It was recognized by colonial government that while a general and elementry knowledge is of value to their effects, it is not in itself sufficient to enable them to carry out research, even if they had time and opportunity. But the governments have often seconded officers in their services, who have received further training in anthropology and have often shown an aptitude for research to make important studies in their territories.

Some of the important studies have been in this way the most remarkable being the research embodied in the series of volumes by Rattray on the Ashanti Gold Coast. Valuable work of the same kind was also done by Dr. Meek in Nigeria and by J.E. Williams and E.W. Pearson Chinnery in New Guinea, W.V. Grigson, an I.C.S. Officer, in India, during the British regime, also ventured to make a similar study of the Bastar people, in his *Maria Gonds of Bastar*. It can be admitted however that even at their best the writings of these administrator-anthropologists seldom satisfy the professional scholars.

Application of Anthropological Knowledge by Different Governments

Having discussed the field of application in which anthropological knowledge can be of much help, let us now see how far and which of the colonial Governments have applied the anthropological knowledge in practice.

Some work of really pragmatic value in the anthropological government had been undertaken by the governments of various country. The government of Anglo-Egyptian Sudan has financed expeditions by professional anthropologists to carry out research, or to employ them on short term contracts for the same purpose, and with intervals research has been going on in that country by Professor and Mrs. Seligman, Dr. Nadel, E.E. Evans – Pritchard and Mr. Lainhardt from 1909 to the present time. This method employed by the Anglo-Egyptian government has the special advantage that while the anthropologist is gaining experience which will later enable him to take a university post. The government was getting it inquiries made by a fully trained man acquainted with the most recent developments in the subject.

Since the last war, the colonial office has also tried to do much in the direction of the anthropological research in the colonial territories, and has financed a large number of students for that. But this means of getting research done has not been entirely successful. As Evans-Pritchard suggests in this connection that research is best carried out through university departments, who select and train the student, while also entrusted with his supervision and guidance. The present policy of the colonial office is to organise the research through local research institutes. One of these, the Rhodes-Livingston Institute in Northern Rhodesia, has been operating since 1938, and three new institutes for social research have been recently founded, one at Maxerere in Uganda, a second at Ibadan in Nigeria, and a third in Jamaica. Besides these, the Government of Great Britain has opened many British Institutes at Rome, Athens and Ankara.

It can be little doubted that in all such anthropological studies and research, launched by the colonial governments and the administrators, the aim has been to promote better understanding of the native people in order to govern them better, though it may not have met its ends as yet fully.

The help of anthropological knowledge was also taken by the African Government, which was faced by a great problem of administering the large number of natives whose customs and practices it could not altogether neglect, nor could it lay aside its principles of justice and equity. The example of a successful intervention by an anthropologist in Africa is very well known. The tribe in question had an ancient custom by which a young man was required to produce a human skull to prove his valour in order to claim a maiden's hand in marriage. To meet the ends of justice in a new socio-political set-up it had become essential that such customs should be abandoned, but the natives were not ready to surrender their age-old custom. The problem could not be solved by a police expedition, but by the helpful intervention of an anthropologist who succeeded in persuading the tribal peoples to substitute the human skull with a wild boar's head. Edwin W. Smith has described in his *Golden Stool* a significant instance of the practical value of anthropological understanding of native customs. Absence of such understanding had already caused much trouble, for the Ashanti people felt offended at the proposed desecration of their sacred relic, the *Golden Stool*, which they used to regard as the soul of their nation. Ratray's intervention saved the situation from taking an ugly turn which would have resulted into a sad massacre between the ruler and the ruled. "Such examples of the triumph of practical anthropology can be multiplied from almost all the sectors of the tribal world" in the words of S.C. Dubey.

The African Government has understood the significant role of native societies in their own context, and had very well realised that any oppression of their laws or customs would result into a bitter fight with the primitive and the so-called "civilized" world. With the realisation of this fact, an *Indirect Rule* came out in Africa, which guaranteed some protection to the native life. The system of Indirect Rule has been built on the assumption that 'native institutions' work by themselves and with fore-sighted planning can be made an effective instrument to bridge the gulf between the rulers and the ruled. In his *Magnum Opus*, Lord Hailey has used. Indirect Rule to denote the system by which the tutelary power recognizes existing African societies and assists them to adopt themselves to the functions of local self-government. Explaining the motives at the back of the "Indirect Rule", Malinowski says that they "are partly those of expediency and efficiency and partly enlightened liberalism". In further support of it he adds, "It is cheap, it is practical and it promises to produce a minimum of friction and dissatisfaction, for it involves rule with the consent of the majority of those governed, and in the maintenance of as much as possible of the native authority instead of its destruction". Given the right soil, Indirect Rule has infinite possibilities of showing results. It grants political authority of those agencies and individuals, whom convention regards as its rightful owner.

Following much the pattern of Indirect Rule, though another variant of it, is the Indianist policy of U.S.A. The Indianist policy sought to make some more reservations for the Indian tribes. The aim of this policy was not to prevent assimilation but to help those who were unable to stand the competition and speed of modern life. It provided for a specialized type of education suited to the needs of the tribes themselves. Judging by its achievements the policy can be said to have succeeded admirably.

United States adopted anthropological knowledge in some other fields also. Though anthropologists in the United States have been drawn more slowly into this type of work than those of countries like Great Britain and the Netherlands, which have more excessive overseas territories. Nevertheless it may be fairly claimed that the pioneer step in this direction was taken by the United States government with the establishment of the Bureau of American Ethnology to study the Indian peoples, then in a "quasi-colonial status". In the Philippines too, one of the first moves of American authorities after taking control from Spain was to set up a Philippines Ethnological Survey to study the archipelago as a basis for governing them successfully.

Dutch colonial administrators have made the most comprehensive and systematic use of anthropology in administration faced by the great diversity of people in the Netherland Indies, they have made the science an essential subject in their training programmes for colonial personnel at Leiden and Utrecht Universities.

Anthropological research supplementary to administration had been carried forward vigorously in the colonial areas under both government and private auspices.

In New Zealand, studies in anthropology along both practical and academic lines have received their strongest support from the Polynesian Maori peoples. Anthropology has been introduced as a subject in training institutes for teachers in New Zealand's native schools, though no systematic training for administrators going to its tropical territories has yet been undertaken. In these South Pacific Lands the limits to applied anthropology have been less in enthusiasm than in finance which has kept personnel and study far from the minimum desired.

The last World War had given tremendous impetus to the application of the anthropological viewpoint. Professional anthropologists have been drawn direct into work both by the Government and University auspices with their main attention focussed on the colonial battle fronts. So also have they been busy in reconstruction after the world war.

Turning our attention to India itself, we find that the work done in this direction in our own country, does not lack in quantity than elsewhere in Asia or even some parts of Europe. The use of anthropological knowledge has been made not only in case of administration or education but also for the "tribal rehabilitation". This work of tribal rehabilitation was given much attention with the achievement of freedom. The national government now finds itself entrusted with the charge of tribal welfare, tribal education, tribal reservations and tribal development. Various tribal centres have been opened both by the central and the principal governments to look into the native and tribal-welfare interests, to solve their problems and to enlighten and educate them, and above all to protect them against all encroachments on their cultures and against forced adoption of any organized system from time to time. To emphasize these, in which apart from the anthropologists from all over the country, tribal representatives participate and discuss some of the tribal problems. One such tribal centres was recently held in Bastar at Jagdalpur in the month of last March.

The Constitution of India guarantees safeguard to the tribal interest. Article 244 of the Constitution of India outlines the "new deal", the Republic has for its tribal populations. The fifth schedule contains provisions which shall apply to the administration and control of the Scheduled Areas and Scheduled Tribes in all states of the Republic except Assam. The provisions regarding the administration of Tribal Areas in Assam are contained in the Sixth Schedule of the Constitution. The Fifth Schedule gives a measure of protection to the tribal populations while the Sixth Schedule by establishing Autonomous Regions in Assam has sought to establish a sort of Indirect Rule there.

The Government, moreover, has the reservations for the tribes in the assemblies as well as in the services. Almost every advertisement for some government has some seats reserved for the tribal candidates, mostly in States which have a noticeable tribal population such as Assam and Madhya Pradesh.

Missionaries particularly in India got much help from the anthropological knowledge in their work of native conversion to Christianity. Many missionaries had taken deep interest in anthropology, for they had realised its value for their own work. They had come to realize that in order to acquaint a native with the 'holy principles of Bible' and in order to convince him that Christianity is the only best religion in the world, the preachers themselves had first to understand the native laws, customs and practices, their social life and religion. Thus some of the work of anthropological value was done also by the missionaries, though solely under the zeal for propagation of their own doctrine.

Anthropological Knowledge as Applied in the Field of Physical Anthropology and Genetics

It has been often customary with the writers on applied anthropology to include under their scheme of the scope of applied anthropology, only the work done in the field of social anthropology. But as we will have little reason to disagree with the view that applied anthropology embraces not only the area covered by social anthropology but also that by physical. Hence it has been planned to discuss under this sub-head, the part played by anthropology in practice in the field of physical anthropology which would include also its use by the geneticist and eugenicists.

First of all let us review those points from which anthropology can apply itself to practical application. From the knowledge of anthropology an anthropologist can help government in bringing into practice some of its useful schemes, such as a health, nutrition and improvement of the living standard of life. For example, we may take in case, such as of a tribe or community which has a very poor health among its members, and because of which they are susceptible to various diseases. An anthropologist by his background of such knowledge can with his constant study of the ease in question, find out or detect the racial or hereditary causes, behind, if there are any in that case. The anthropologist can also in the meanwhile suggest some solution to the problem. Among the Jodas of South India, it was noticed that as a result of infant mortality the population was decreasing gradually. The anthropologist went in search of its causes, and suggested that probably the widely practised, polyandry among the Jodas was the cause for this high infant mortality. He framed suggestions, and as they were gradually brought into practice, the decrease in the population tended to be reduced. Hardly anyone else even with his long and constant efforts and labour would have been able to help the situation.

Anthropologist is also of invaluable help to government in helping it to adopt some of its health-schemes, such as of nutrition and raising of health standard. An anthropologist can suggest the minimum desired, and he can also suggest: What are the essential requirements of a particular people as well as how they are to be met with.

The greatest claims made for the application of anthropological knowledge in the field of physical anthropology, are those by Eugenics or what is called "the science of 'breeding better?" Anthropologists of the above line have favoured the view that a study of the fundamental principles of genetics becomes necessary in order to have a fully scientific study of man. A study of genetics furnishes us with the knowledge that some traits are defective and are necessary to be checked. In order to maintain the equilibrium of the racial stock and in order to decrease the number of such cacoganic traits, it becomes necessary that the persons carrying them should be checked from breeding further so that the same hereditary cacoganic traits may not be passed on to the next generation.

Anthropologist cannot only suggest the harmful consequence of such traits, but also against the people with the facts, and convinces them with the necessity of checking them. He, thus, can help the cause by his simple study and efforts, what the government would have failed to despite all its laws and regulations, for they would only result into utter dissatisfaction.

This has also been brought into force in some of the western countries, where the government with the aid of anthropologists has been able to check the evil-effects by spread of defective traits. Though in certain cases this knowledge may also be misapplied, such as criminals and traitors may be sterilised for the fear that they may increase their numbers by breeding. But as is clear, this is not based on a sound study of the subject, for it would be clear with such characters as crime and offence are not hereditary. But this does not reduce the importance of the application of anthropological knowledge to this field, for misuse or mis-application is possible in case of almost all branches of knowledge.

The eugenicists have also advanced their claims in a positive direction by their programme for "breeding better". This positive eugenics aims to suggest the desirable traits which ought to be spread in order to improve the racial stock. It is just likely that experiments in this way have also been made.

Anthropological knowledge has also been made use of in throwing light on an age-old controversy over the issue – whether inbreeding is harmful and results in the deterioration of the stock or not. By study and research in this field, anthropologists now, more or less, are agreed over the fact that inbreeding is not always bad. It is bad in case the inbreeding stock is bad, but also good in case the stock is good, for inbreeding, as Hoebell remarks, does nothing more than "intensify the dominant traits". This knowledge has been of much use and help to the anthropologists and ethnologists.

Besides, these the use of anthropological knowledge is made also by the traders and big concerns such as a company of ready-made clothes. An anthropologist can give an average size of the clothes for a fixed population, as he knows their average size and stature.

In India, the role of applied anthropology had been limited, though not altogether negligent, before the achievement of independence. There were few anthropologists who could make efforts in the direction of practical efforts. Government too had not paid much heed to this subject. However Dr. D.N. Majumdar, was once called as late as in 1943, by the then government to acquaint the I.C.S. trainees with an anthropological outlook. He was invited to give them some lectures on the anthropology in India. With this we find that even the British Government had to realize in the administration, though this was realised at a quite late stage. Anyhow, with the national government in the country this has now got a sufficient consideration and much is being done in this direction both by the Government and the anthropologist in India. Several research centres are now training administrators in tribal administration.

Applied Anthropology as an Aid in other Fields

Applied anthropology is used not only by the administrators and colonial governments to solve the problem between the rulers and the ruled natives but it proves of immense help to other fields of study and sciences also, besides those discussed above. It helps to solve the problems of native laws and customs (as illustrated above by a practical example of Ashanti people in Africa); in native education, – native economics, land tenure and native health, as well as in ascertaining the position of native women. The case for native laws and customs, has already been discussed above, so also with regard to the native education. He will examine here thus in brief the contribution of anthropological knowledge to native economics, land tenure, and native health.

Native Economics

Since the war, a great revolution has been in progress with regard to native trading methods. Even before the war, the Indian *banias* in East Africa, Syria and at other places on the west coast were banking down the old indigenous outlook to trade. Advances in crops not yet harvested were being introduced. This produced such undesirable results that "A restriction credit to native ordinances" was introduced into Uganda. In Kenya, a proposal to protect natives by a similar ordinance was introduced on the grounds that it was better for the natives to learn the disadvantages by bitter experiences. The general failure of the native-owned retail store needed further investigation. Anthropologists were trying to help the situation.

Land Tenure

Anthropologists have been helping the government in Africa to fix rules for land tenure. The area necessary for each family also need special study, now that agricultural departments are urging the culture of economic crops in the reserves and also endeavouring to introduce improving farming methods.

Native Health

Anthropologists is of much aid in case of native-health problems also. The curing of the disease is the function of the doctor, but even the help of the administrator is especially required in order to persuade the natives that Western medicine is the best to cure their disease, and to insure "native" co-operation. In the matter of native nutrition, the help of the administrator is particularly needed. In the field of hygiene, the doctor is powerless without the support of the district offices and the educationist, who in turn get much help and guidance in the matter from an experienced or trained anthropologist. This may seem outside the sphere of even practical anthropology, but not so; for it is essential to ascertain what old customs, what old prejudices stand in the way of the adoption of better hygienic methods.

Thus we find that the limits of the field of anthropological study in application are very broad and extensive. With the growing of complex situations and hardening of human relations, the chances of anthropological study are growing better. The world in need of one or the other practical solution for one, or the other human problem would continue to look at the anthropologist as it knows well that it is only he who understands, or better to say, tries to understand mankind "better". The scope of applied anthropology thus would go on widening and extending till it reaches its limits which are hard to ascertain at present.

Anthropological knowledge proves of much help in the field of medical ethnology as well as in Eugenics. From the knowledge gained from the study of genetics and biology, it can prescribe rules to check the inbreeding of the undesired persons carrying defective traits, as seen above. Here also it helps much both to the individual as well as to the state.

As has been put so beautifully by Evans-Pritchard:

> "In the changed situations of today technical experts have become increasingly important in our colonial empire, the doctor, the agricultural officer, the forestry officer, the veterinary officer, the engineer and so on, and also the trades and representatives of mining and other business interests. At present most of them are expected to carry out their various jobs among whose way of life and ideas they often know next to nothing.
>
> A question at this point can be raised – "how the knowledge of anthropology helps Europeans (or other ruling powers) in their dealings with the native peoples?"

For a long time anthropologists have spoken about "applied anthropology" much as one speaks about applied medicine or engineering. But it should be remembered that those who have spoken so have regarded anthropology as a natural science, which aims at the establishment of laws of social life; and once theoretical generalizations can be established, applied anthropology becomes feasible. It would be clear from what has been said above that this normative element in anthropology is like the concept of natural law and progress, from which it derives part of its heritage. It had been customary with the eighteenth century philosophers, nineteenth century ethnologists and majority of the social anthropologists of today, to take natural sciences for their model, and they assumed that the purpose of anthropology is by prediction and planning to control social change. This assumption is summed up in the phrase – "social engineering." But as we know this is not wholly true. Anthropology cannot lay down general and universal laws, since mankind are subject to differ from place to place, and time to time. Under such conditions anthropology can be the science only in the sense in which history is a science.

Summarising the scope of applied anthropology we can very well say that a knowledge of anthropology helps a person in every walk of his life and wherever he goes. As we have discussed above the anthropologist is of utmost help to the State in the service of the tribal populations. By his work, an anthropologist not only helps the government, but also makes himself of much service of the natives – for the solution of urgent and pressing problems rising now and then in the administration of tribal areas, the anthropologist with his intimate knowledge of the tribes, their ideas, attitudes and value structures can be very useful. His services in establishing first contacts between the people and the government can indeed be important. In periods of crisis, such as, rise of aggressive cults, mass killings and general disobedience to law and order, he cannot only advise the government on the best approach but can effectively use his contacts and influence on both sides for bringing about a mutually profitable agreement. For the formation of the laws of tenure, and in general for establishing a basis of economic and political co-operation, his services can be invaluable. Through him administration can learn how to assess properly the value of native evidence. In everyday administration an officer with an anthropological background and perspective is decidedly an asset. In tribal-cultures isolated question can be properly understood only against the background of the whole social life in the context of their total culture.

Anthropology builds up this much needed background information. To quote Beaglehole,

> The inoculation of administrators and officials with the anthropological point of view contributes immeasurably to a more efficient tolerant, enlightened, and sympathetic government of the native peoples concerned. The educator, the missionary, the administrator, need anthropological sophistication if their relations with native peoples are to be fruitful and friendly, the citizen needs the same informed knowledge if he is to be critically aware of the policies and methods that rule the relation of his state to the native peoples in its charge.

Anthropologists today have also claimed the application of their findings to other affairs, – the emphasis in England being on colonial problems, while in America, on political and industrial problems. Some of its more reasonable advocates, have, however, held that there can only be applied social anthropology when the 'science of man' is much more advanced than it is today; but we find even so eminent an authority as Professor Radcliffe Brown writing:

> With the more rapid advance of the pure science itself, and with the development of colonial administrations, we might even look forward to a time when the government and education of native peoples in various parts of the world would make some approach to being an art based on the discovered laws of anthropological science.

Moreover, it is also to be noted that more popular writers on anthropology especially in America, have made far reaching claims for immediate application of anthropological knowledge in 'social planning'.

In conclusion, we can say that the study of applied anthropology enables us from one angle to see mankind as a whole. When we get accustomed to the anthropological way of looking at human cultures and societies, we move easily from the particular to the general and back again. Only by understanding other cultures and societies, does one see one's own in perspective, and comes to understand it better against a background of the totality of human experience and endeavour; as Margaret Mead gained some understanding in Samoa of American problems of adolescence; Malinowski shed light on problems of incentives in British industry by his study of Trobriand Islanders and their system of exchange of ritual objects, and Evans Pritchard gained some understanding of Communist Russia by studying witchcraft among the Azande. To sum this all, we can say with Evans-Pritchard, that "the knowledge of social anthropology, helps us to understand better, and at whatever place or time we meet him, that wondrous creature man."

An estimation of the scope of applied anthropology can thus be attempted in the above light on the subject, though limits to it cannot be ascertained with growing field of knowledge, and its widening application to various fields.

14

The Theories of Primitive Religion

RELIGION is a mystical concept both for the savage and the civilized alike. Religion has a strong influence on the individual. For the primitive man it has a still greater influence. The religious life of any people is expressed in manifestations in outer forms, in beliefs and in rites.

Durkheim, therefore, defined religion as composed of "beliefs and rites"; beliefs about sacred things and rites addressed to them. Beliefs according to him are static, while rituals are dynamic. Mere beliefs do not constitute religion, it is rites which make religion a living force.

Durkheim does not attempt to define religion, since he holds that religion cannot be defined, but can only be understood with regard to its subject matter. He regards religion to be separate from magic, as the former is, according to him, sacred, and the latter profane.

Tylor, another distinguished writer, defined religion as a "belief in spiritual beings". From this he develops his animistic theory of religion.

Maxmuller, the German scholar and exponent of the Naturalism, defined religion as a "a longing or desire to know the unknown, the unknowable and understandable, i.e., the "infinite".

Without engrossing ourselves in any detailed discussion of what religion is and what it is not, we shall confront ourselves with some of the basic theories of religion which have been put forward. Thus we shall be discussing here three main theories – Animism, Naturism and Manaism.

Animism

Animism, as a theory of religion in social anthropology means "belief in spiritual beings". Animism as such is associated with Tylor, the originator of the animistic doctrine.

Under the name of Animism, Edward B. Tylor, attempts to investigate the deep-lying doctrine of Spiritual Beings, which embodies the very essence of Spiritualistic as opposed to Materialistic philosophy, as he himself tells us. "The sense of spiritualism in its wider acceptation, the general belief in spiritual being, as Tylor says, "is here given to Animism. The term 'Animism' is derived from "anima" a Latin word, which means "soul". Hence Tylor also defines Animism as a philosophy of soul. He holds animism to be the earliest form of religious life. Animism, he maintains, characterizes tribes very low in the scale of humanity, and thence ascends, deeply modified in its transmission, but from first to last preserving an unbroken continuity, into the midst of high modern culture. Animism is, in fact, according to Tylor, "the groundwork of the Philosophy of Religion, from that of savages upto that of civilized men".

And although it may at first sight seem to afford, but a bare and meager definition of religion, it will be found, is practically sufficient, "for where the root is, the branches will generally be produced", remarks Tylor in his *Primitive Culture* (1873).

It is found that the theory of Animism divides into two great dogmas, forming parts of one consistent doctrine; first concerning souls of individual creatures, capable of continued existence after the destruction of the body; second concerning other spirits, upward to the rank of powerful deities. Spiritual Beings are held to affect or control the events of the material world, and man's life here and hereafter; and it being considered that they hold intercourse with men, and receive pleasure or displeasure from human actions, the belief in their existence leads naturally, and it might almost be said inevitably, sooner or later to active reverence and propitiation. Thus, Animism in its full development includes the belief in souls and in a future state, in controlling deities and subordinate spirits, these doctrines practically resulting in some kind of active worship. Tylor says while proposing to discuss the animistic theory he proposes hardly to touch upon the purely moral aspects of religion, but rather to study the animism of the world so far as it constitutes an ancient and world-wide philosophy of which belief is the theory and worship is the practice.

For a long time, we see, Animism was regarded as the sole religion of tribes in India, but now the nomenclature is changed to 'tribal religion', it being found that Animism does not exhaust all that religion consists of.

Tylor then proceeds to define the spirit as follows. A spirit, according to the dictionaries, as we well know, may be identified with any supernatural being, good or bad, and the term has been very often used in the various writings.

It is commonly conceded that the spiritual represents the opposite of material existence.

Tylor proceeds to explain the concept of Spirit through that of soul. "Soul" is the keynote in Tylor's scheme of religion. It is the essence of his animistic theory. Tylor assumes the concept of soul to be "the philosophy of the double."

The difficulty is, as Lowie reminds, that if we insist on the notion of completely incorporeal being, there are probably no examples to be found on primitive levels. Certainly none appears in the beliefs of the tribes hitherto described. Nevertheless some of these belong to a different order of existence from that of a man, beasts and rocks. They are not indeed immaterial, but they are certainly less grossly material from the bodies of ordinary physical objects, and it is this subtler mode of existence that may be called "spiritual" in an ethnological sense.

The primitive people develops a philosophy of the double. The Negrito of the Andaman Islands in the Bay of Bengal have the highly typical belief that man has a soul in the form of a breath, double, reflection, or shadow, which can leave its owner during his sleep and travel far away.

After the destruction of a person's body, it is this 'double' that departs, becoming a spirit either of the jungle or of the sea. Spirits are attacked by whistling but kept away by singing also by a fire-brand or a human bone.

Another description of soul is that given by the Shashoni of Idaho, which finds it as "ten inches tall", and is washed. "As Lowie says, a soul that is washed, a soul that is ten inches tall does not correspond to our notion of Spirituality. Yet it is obvious that the Shoshoni (a primitive people) conceive it as distinct and of fine essence than the human body."

Tylor says, "the soul of the primitive man is a thin unsubstantial image, in its nature a sort of vapour, film or shadow." Abundant linguistic evidence could be adduced to prove that it is usually designated by terms somehow denoting this finer type of materiality. Thus, according to Tylor, all primitive men believe in soul and they regard some part of the body as the centre of the soul; some regarding the heart, liver or blood as the centre of the soul. In many regions of the globe, there is a dual-soul concept, i.e., a belief in two or even more souls.

Some peoples even attribute four souls to every human body, as is the belief among the Yuchi. A quadruple soul has also been recorded among the Dakota.

The Kamars of Chhatisgarh in India also have a faith in the spirit-philosophy. According to the Kamar-belief, after the destruction of a person's body, his *jeev* or soul goes to the God and his body becomes *madhee.* The soul is invited to live with the ancestor spirits. It may also take re-birth. The *madhe* dwells in the graveyard and is a potent source of trouble. The dream experiences of an individual are the true encounters of his soul. Starting from this point the imaginative mind of man develops an elaborate theory of animism, and comes to view the world, as a place full to countless spirits of numerous varieties. To the Kamars, rocks, mountains, rivers and trees are not without a spirit. Some of these spirits react favourably or unfavourably to different type of human acts. According to Majumdar, the Korwas of Mirzapur believe that crops, cattle and rain have all their presiding-spirits. Animism as a feature of primitive religion is to be found widely distributed all over the world.

The problem that arises now is that how does the primitive man come to have the knowledge about the soul. The origin of the popular conception of soul, Tylor attempts to discover in dreams, visions and other such states of consciousness.

Tylor's scheme thus naturally divides itself as in to two parts – First, he determines how the concept of comparatively spiritual as opposed to grossly material existence could ever have arisen; secondly, he attempts to show, when that concept had once evolved how 'all' types of supernatural beings evolved from it.

Each enquiry can be best considered separately, we will be thus seeing – how the concept of spirit came to the knowledge of primitive man which helped him to develop the idea of the double which was elaborated later into animism.

The Origin of the Spirit Concept

According to Tylor, the belief in a more refined form of existence than the bodily one of normal experience is based both on an inference from observed facts and on the direct evidence of the senses. Primitive man, by his observation and experience notices a difference between the living body and the corpse, and from this he concludes that there must be something in the formers however elusive in essence, that is absent in the latter; hence the notion of a vital principle.

But secondly, the savage sees, Tylor goes it on to suggest, either in dreams or in visionary revelations, human shapes different from those of waking experience. "When the sleeper awakens from a dream, he believes he has really somehow been away; or that other people have come to him". But since his body lies where he lay down to rest, since the people he sees are known to be far away, it is necessarily not his normal self or selves of his dream interlocutors that are concerned, but phantom selves presenting a new category of reality, though wearing the semblance of the fleshy body, suggests Tylor.

At one place in his *Primitive Culture*, he remarks: "My own view is that nothing but dreams or visions could ever have put in to men's mind such an idea as that of souls being ethereal images of bodies."

Tylor tells us that the primitive man sees shadows and tries to catch them, but cannot. From this he begins to think that it is something which he cannot catch, and thus develops the idea of double. "His reflections in tanks, his echoes in forests, the dreams he sees, all help him in developing the idea of the double. These things are elusive and the primitive man tries to grapple with these ideas".

The primitive man thinks, this 'double' can temporarily leave the body, as it does in dreams, and re-enter it as when the man is awake. In the words of Tylor himself:

> "The ghost or phantom seen by the dreamer or the visionary is an unsubstantial form, like a shadow, and thus the familiar term for the shadow is also that for the spirit in many primitive tribes".

Tylor illustrates this from a number of examples from the Tasmanians, the Zulus and the Alogonquin Indians, where the term 'shadow' is synonymous with that for the 'soul'.

We note thus that when Tylor had answered the question, how humanity ever came to receive such a thing as spirit at all, and next confronted the varied manifestations of belief in Supernatural Being he automatically attempted to bring order into a welter of facts, by a theory monistic in its psychology and unilinear in its historical implications.

The vital force and the phantom are intimately connected with the body, the former enabling it to feel, think and act, while the latter is its image or double. Further, both are the separable from the body, the life principle during insensibility or destruction; the double as it appears to people at a distance. Tylor argues that primitive man combines the two into the notion of a ghost soul. Given the human soul, the extension of the soul concept to other animals was natural considering the primitive view of animals as not basically distinct from man. As for the souls attributed to inanimate objects, Tylor points out that even they may be regarded as endowed with life, while in any event they will appear as phantoms in dreams and visions alongside of persons, wearing, carrying, or otherwise using them.

Let us now understand here the relation of Tylor's theory to the phenomenon to which it pertains. The starting point of inquiry is that even the extremely rude tribes, believe in the existence of a spiritual, that is relatively immaterial reality. Now, how they acquired this belief, was the problem before Tylor, to which he himself puts the question. And as he had himself put the question, he also brought forth a ready-made answer. He says that the lack of an empirical basis is only apparent, and he cites two sets of phenomena that conjointly may have led to the notion of spirit as here defined. He has no pretensions of having any historical records for the origin of a conception that belongs to dim antiquity.

Theory of Nature and Sequence of Supernatural Beings

The second aspect of Tylor's theory of Animism is a Nature and sequence of Supernatural Beings. In the words of Lowie, "Tylor represented in admirable fashion the characteristics of the English intellect".

Tylor in laying out money of his theories was but following the tradition of his time, i.e., the derivation of evolutionary ideas from the biological field. The biologists were asserting that an essential unity underlay the apparent diversity of organic life; and the varied forms of religious life were linked likewise by a fundamental likeness. When Tylor had answered the question how humanity ever came to conceive such a thing at all, and next confronted the varied manifestations of belief in supernatural-beings, he automatically attempted to bring order into a welter of facts by a theory monistic in its psychology and unilinear in its historical implications. As to the psychological interpretation, Tylor says:

> It seems as though the conception of a human soul, whence once attained to by man, served as a type or model on which he framed not only his ideas of other souls of lower grade, but also his ideas of spiritual beings in general, from the times self that sports in the long grass up to the heavenly creator and Rules of the World, the Great Spirit.

Spirit

Tylor at another place remarks:

> "The idea of souls, demons, deities, and any other classes of spiritual beings are conceptions of similar nature, throughout, the conceptions of souls being the original ones of the series".

In part the argument on behalf of this basic unity seems quite convincing. It is easy to understand how the souls of living, postulated for reasons set forth in the first part of Tylor's scheme, should assume the character of malignant demons or benign patrons after the destruction of the body.

There is also a good deal to be said for the interpretation of what Tylor calls "fetichism" as the human soul can exist in the human body or leave it, in dream life and abnormal states, so spirits modelled on the soul many either flit about freely or become sacred objects of "fetiches".

As to the alleged identity of nature spirits with human souls, Tylor says: "As the human body was held to live and act by virtue of its own inhabiting spirit – soul, so the operations of the world seem to be carried on by the influence of other spirits". These spirits are looked upon as souls working nature much as human souls work human bodies. Thus the 'firmament' is explained by an undwelling deity, modelled on the human soul. We may best understand what was meant by the Heaven God if we think of him as the soul of the sky.

As first, the spirits are merged in their element, later as anthropomorphic gods, they are independent controllers of the phenomenon. Undoubtedly the facts can be explained along these lines. But if we ask, whether Tylor had demonstrated his interpretative principle to the exclusion of all others, it must be said that no such rigid proof is to be bound.

Thus we find that Tylor accounts for the origin of the spirit concept and the birth of the philosophy of Animism.

In the opinion of Majumdar,

> The change of soul into spirit is the greatest event in human cultural history and it is at the destruction of the body, that such transformation or metamorphosis could take place.

The tribal religions of India have so long been described as animism, but this is not true in case of all the tribal religion, though many of them may be animistic. "Animism is that exceedingly crude form of religion in which magic is the predominant element". It conceives of man as passing through a life surrounded by ghostly campaign of powers, elements, mostly impersonal in their character, 'shapeless phantom of which no image can be made, and no definite idea can be formed. Animism carries with it the belief in malevolent spirits and powers, which influence the destiny of man.

Having discussed 'Animism' – as a theory of religion – let us now proceed to examine it critically.

A Critical Examination of Animistic Theory

Animism, as we have seen, has been defined by Tylor as "a belief in spiritual beings".

Though, this theory of religion was based on sound logical principles, yet it could not escape the criticism directed against it by several authors.

The main objection to Tylor's scheme of animism was raised by Durkheim.

First of all, Durkheim directs his criticism against Tylor's dream phenomena from which he derives his "Spirit" concept which forms the basis of his whole philosophy of religion.

"Why", asks the French scholar, "should primitive man crave a theoretical interpretation of dream life? He is not a philosopher who deliberately connects theories of the phenomena he observed".

1. This seems a right point to attack at. It does not seem probable that a primitive man may raise questions about such a complicated phenomena as dream. The phenomena of dream is not even properly interpreted by the most civilized of the men. How could then a primitive man, wandering in his ignorance as he does, come to formulate such a theoretical interpretation of the dream life.

2. Secondly, we find, as Lowie has remarked: "Tylor's formulation is not exacting enough for it omits an essential determinant of the phenomena 'o be defined" yet in another sense. We find, meager as it may appear at first sight, it demands more than is required".

3. Lowie further points out that the fact that subjective states indistinguishable from religious ones are indifferently found with and without animistic notion, definitely settles the matter. We shall, therefore, recognize as the differentia of religions he says, what Marett and Goldenweiser have called "supernaturalism".

Reverting to the problem that engaged. Tylor's attention, we can say, "Religion is verily a universal feature of human culture, not because all societies foster a belief in spirits, but because all recognize in some form or other, awe-inspiring, extra-ordinary manifestations of reality. Owing to many ramifications of such supernaturalism, this definition of religion leads not, we find, to rigid exclusion but merely to a somewhat different appraisal of features commonly treated under the head of religion. Lowie points out that for the colourless terms employed above.

Soderblour substitutes the concept of the Holy or the Sacred, but it would not be a very exact usage, as he himself further tells us.

What more recent scholars reject thus, we find, is not conclusion itself but the motivation in Tylor's philosophy of religion.

In Tylor's discussion, the belief in Spiritual beings, that is, religion in his sense is made to arise in response to an "intellectual needs" the desire of an explanation for the physiological phenomena of nature life, dream and mortal end.

His rationalistic bias appears clearly from the very phrases used in referring to primitive animism, which is again and again alluded as a philosophy, a doctrine, "the theory of souls".

It is conceivable that a craving for causal explanation might lead to the notion of spirits as suggested by Tylor without the slightest consequent or associated emotional reaction essential to religion; indeed not a few examples might be cited of spiritual beings postulated by primitive tribes for, so far as one can see, an exclusive satisfaction of their metaphysical demands.

Tylor's phraseology is often tinctured with rationalistic psychologizing, but as Lowie tells us, "Durkheim does not put his finger on the right spot". Tylor is in fault so far as he limits the consideration of religion almost wholly to the beliefs in spiritual beings, that is, to the 'conceptual' respect of religion without due regard to its emotional concomitants. But in the present context, the charge of intellectualism is pointless, because Tylor is concerned with tracing the origin of a concept, that is, of a cognition element of consciousness. Further he derives it very largely not from ratiocination about observed phenomena, but from the immediate sensory of testimony of dream life.

Tylor's theory is avowedly a psychological interpretation, pure and simple, but as Lowie is also ready to admit, as much as it not only explains the empirical observations but operates exclusively, with facts like dreams, visions and mortal end, all of which demonstrably exercise a strong influence on the minds of primitive men, it must be conceded to have a high degree of probability.

Marett also made objections to Tylor's animistic theory, as he maintained that both animism and animatism (a term which he himself coined) are essentially non-religious, or only potentially religious, becoming religious only in so far as the emotional attitude characteristics of religious clusters about their objects are concerned.

Ruth Benedict called 'animism' – "a confusion between two of our most carefully separate categories, the animate and inanimate".

As regards Durkheim's objections raised against Tylor's animism, we find that they leave Tylor's explanation entirely unshaken. Certainly, the alternative proposed by the critic cannot be regarded as an adequate substitute.

In conclusion, we can say that Tylor's contribution made in the field of religion is not without value. The theory of religion, as "a belief in spiritual beings", may not seem as a tangible explanation of religion to many, but few would deny that it contains an essential element of truth at its core by emphasising the part spirit thoughts may have played in the development of religious-concept and as such is readily an advance over many other explanations of religion.

Manaism

Belief in religion is not universally the same, but it may assumes different forms in different societies.

Manaism is also a belief in some kind of Supernaturalism. This Manaism is most common in Melanesia, though it is scattered in other parts of the world also.

Codrington defines 'mana', in its Melanesian use, as follows: "a force altogether distinct from physical power, which acts all kinds of ways for good and evil, and which it is of the greatest advantage to possess or control". Or again as he says: "It is a power of influence, not physical, and in a way supernatural; but it shows itself in physical force, or in any kind of power or excellence a man possesses". It is supernatural just in this way, namely, that it is "what works to effect everything which is beyond the ordinary power of men, outside the common processes of nature. He illustrates this point by examples:

> "If a man has been successful in fighting, it has not been his natural strength of arm, quickness of eye, or readiness of resource that has won success; he has certainly got the

'mana' of a spirit or some deceased warrior to empower him, conveyed in an amulet of a stone round his neck or a tuft of leaves in his belt, in a tooth hung upon a finger of his bow hand, or in the form of woods with which he brings supernatural assistance to his side. If a man's pigs multiply, and his gardens are productive, it is not because he is industrious and looks after his property, but because of the stones full of 'mana' for pigs and yams that he possesses. Of course a yam naturally grows when planted that is well known, but it will not be large unless 'mana' comes into play; a canoe will not be swift unless 'mana' be brought to bear upon it, a net will not catch many fish, nor an arrow inflict a mortal wound.

From Polynesia also comes much the same story. Treager in his admirable comparative dictionary of the Polynesian dialects renders the word which many be either noun or adjective, thus: "supernatural power: divine authority; having qualities, which ordinary persons or things do not possess". He seems to distinguish however, what might be called a "secular" sense, in which the term stands generally for "authority", or as an adjective, for "effectual effective". He cites copious instance from the various dialects to exemplify the supernatural mode of 'mana'. Thus the word is applied in Maori, to a wooden sword that has done deeds so wonderful as to possess a sanctity and power of its own; a Samoan, to a parent who brings a curse on a disobedient child in Hawaiian, to the gods, or to a man after the destruction of his body, gives efficacy to an idol.

It may in some cases be applied to a magic stuff, or again to a divination in general, and so forth.

In short, its range is as wide as those of divinity and witchcraft taken together.

Thus the concept of *Mana* is quite extensive and may include all kinds of supernatural varieties.

The concept of *Mana* was given much emphasis, or rather we can call it to have originated in social anthropology with R.R. Marett. He has expounded the theory in his *Threshold of Religion*.

If on the other hand, we turn, Marett tells us, to what he has called the secular sense attributed to *mana*, for example, when it is used of a chief, a healer of maladies, a successful pleader, or the winner of a race, we perceive at once that the distinction of meaning holds good for the civilized lexicographer rather than for the unsophisticated native.

Thus we find that all the examples quoted above that throughout the Pacific religion, *mana* in its essential meaning connotes what both Codrington and Treages describe as the Supernatural.

Now let us proceed to examine, what other important forms does this *manaism* assumes, or to what other forms of supernatural beliefs it is similar.

Animatism, we find is another kind of belief in supernaturalism found in several primitive cultures of the world. Among the Melanesians, as we have seen, it is called *mana*. The tribes of Chhota Nagpur call it *Bonga*. In the other parts of the world, it is variously described as *Wakonda* or *Orenda*.

About *Wakande* or *the Siouan waken*, as M'Gee writes : the term may be translated into 'mystery' perhaps more satisfactorily than in any other single English word, yet this rendering is at the same time too limited, as *wakanda* vaguely denotes also power, sacred, ancient, grandeur, animate, immortal. Amongst such notions, Marett writes, that of "the supernatural" stands, as the least objectionable. The savage has no word for "nature". He does not abstractly distinguish between an order of uniform happenings and a higher order of miraculous happenings.

According to this conception, a non-material, impersonal and non-individualized power pervades things. It can manifest itself in both animate and inanimate things. It can be utilized for attaining specific objective, if it is properly tapped.

As Cordington says:

> A man comes by chance upon a stone which takes his fancy; its shape is singular it is like something, it is certainly not a common stone, there must be *mana* in it. So he argues with himself, and he puts it to the roof, he lays it at the root of a tree to the fruit of which it has a certain resemblance, or he buries it in the ground when he plants his garden; an abundant crop on the tree or in the garden shows that he is right, the stone is *mana*, has that power in it.

It is under such beliefs, that the germs of *manaism* lie and here is the birth of a religious philosophy of *mana*.

Marett adds that in any case, the English word "Supernatural" seems to suit this context better than the word "sacred". Marett also tells that the Latin "sacer" merely amounts to *tabu*, which is the negative model of the supernatural. Thus the term "taboo" also needs a treatment here in order to understand *manaism* fully.

The Concept of Tabu: the Prohibitive Power

Tabu, according to Marett is the negative mode of the supernatural, to which *mana* corresponds as the positive mode. Here Marett does not confine the treatment of the terms only to its Melanesian usage, but in a sense of worldwide application. As Marett writes: "Given to the supernatural in any form there are always two things to note about it: firstly, that you are to be heedful about it; secondly that it has power. The first may be called its negative character, the second its positive".

Tabu it might be argued, is not so much negative as prohibitive, on even miniatory; whilst *mana* is not merely positive but operative, and than maturgic: "Given this wide sense, *tabu* simply implies," further writes Marett, "that you must be heedful in regard to the supernature not that you must be on your guard against it". The warning is against casual, incautions, profane dealings. "Not to be highly approached", is Codrington's translation for the corresponding term used in the New Hebrides. *Tabu*, as popularly used, may in a given context connote something like absolute prohibition, but in the universal application that has been given to it by Marett can only represent the supernatural in its negative character – the supernatural, so to speak, on the defensive.

Thus the relation of *tabu* to *mana* has been shown by Marett to the negative – or rather more precisely 'prohibitive', and positive or operative aspects of the same 'supernatural' belief.

The Positive or Operative *Mana*

We now come to *mana*. *Mana* as we have mentioned, is often 'thaumaturgic', but not always. Like energy, *mana* may be dormant or potential. *Mana* let us remember, is an adjective as well as a noun, expressing a possession which is likewise a permanent quality. The stone that looks like a 'banana' is and has *mana*. Hence it seems enough to say that *mana* exhibits the supernatural in its positive capacity – ready, but not necessarily in act, to strike.

An important consideration arises here, *Tabu* and *mana* apply to the supernatural solely as viewed in what Marett calls its first, or existential dimension. With its second, or moral-dimension they have nothing to do whatever. They register judgments of facts as philosophers would say, not judgments of value; they are constitutive categories, nor normative. Thus whatever is supernatural is indifferently *tabu* – perilous to the unwary; but as such it may equally well be holy or unclean, set apart for God or abandoned to devil, sainted or sinful, cloistered or quanantined.

There is plenty of linguistic evidence to show that such distinctions of value are familiar to the savage mind. Nor is it hard to see how they arise naturally out of the *tabu* idea. Thus in Melanesia everything supernatural is at once 'tambu' and *rongo* – words implying that is fenced round by sanctions human and divine. Passing on to *mana*, we find exactly the same absence of moral significance. The mystic potentiality is alike for good and evil. Thus *mana* and *tale* are only relative terms.

Animism and Manaism

Animism and Manaism both are said to impose a belief in the 'supernatural' power. Then how they differ or what relation do the two have to each other. Put in a nutshell the problem is the following: "How does animism" fit into the scheme? Is the supernatural identical with the spiritual, and is *mana* nothing more or less than spiritual power? Or on the contrary, what are *mana* and *soul* or *spirit* categories that belong to relatively distinct systems of ideas – "do the two refuse to combine?" – as Marett raised the problem. We shall briefly examine this here.

As regards this latter question, we find that some how these categories do manage to combine freely, and notably in that very pacific region. Where *mana* is at home The Melanesian evidence collected by Codrington in his work, *The Melanesians* is decisive.

Wherever *mana* is found and that is to say wherever the supernatural reveals itself, this *mana* is referred to one of three originating sources, namely, a living man, a ghost, or a "spirit"; spirits displaying one of two forms, that of a ghostlike appearance – as a native put it, "something indistinct", with no definite outline, gray like dust, vanishing as soon as looked at" – or that of the ordinary corporeal figure of a man. Finally, animism can be made without much trouble to cover the case of the living man with *mana*.

If a man has *mana*, it resides in his "spiritual part" or "soul", which after him becomes a ghost. Besides, it appears, provable that no man has his power of himself, not that he is *mana*, as we can say of a ghost or spirit.

.Thus we find that *mana* and animism can occur in combination.

It makes no difference whether we take animism in the vaguer Spencerian use of the attribution of life and animation – an attitude of mind to which Marett gives the name of "animatism" – or in the more exact Tylorian sense of the attribution of soul, ghost, or ghost-like spirit. "In either case we are carried far beyond the bounds of rudimentary religious", as Marett tells us; "even when magic is made a co-partner in the system". Mana can come very near to meaning "soul" or "spirit", though without the connotation of wrath-like appearance.

Marett, concludes in emphasizing the relation of mana to animism, that *mana*, or rather the *tabu-mana* formula, has solid advantages over animism, when the avowed object is to find what Tylor calls "a minimum definition" of religion. *Mana* is co-extensive with the supernatural animism is far too wide. *Mana* is always *mana*, supernatural power, differing in intensity – in voltage, to speak – but never is essence; animism, splits up into more or less irreducible kinds, notably "soul", "spirit" and "ghost". Finally, *mana* whilst fully adapted to express the immaterial – the unseen force at work behind the seen, yet, comfortably with the incoherent state of rudimentary reflection, leaves in solution the distinction between personal and impersonal, and in particular, does not allow any notion of a high individuality to be precipitated. Animism, on the other hand, tends to lose touch with the supernatural in its more impersonal forms, and is not well suited to express its transmissibility nor indeed its immateriality; but, by way of compensation, it can, in a specialized form, become a means of representing supernatural agents of high individuality, whenever the social condition of mankind is advanced enough to foster such a conception. Both animism and manaism are quite closely related to each other.

Bongaism

The belief in the supernatural power, or the impersonal force of *Mana* is widely scattered among the primitive religious of the world. Manaism is traced also in the different primitive tribes, such as the Hos of Chhota Nagpur plateau, the Holiyas etc.

Manaism in India has also been a principle cause of the caste-system in high and low caste feelings. It is not difficult to trace endogenous occupational basis, and untouchability, says Majumdar, from the dread of uncanny *mana*. We are told by the competent authorities that it is not the Brahmins alone who avoid the *Holiyas*, (an outcaste people), but the latter must not approach the former without being sure that his influence has become innocuous so far as himself and his material possessions are concerned. That is how, when a Brahmin enters the Paracheny of the Holiyas, men and women from the settlement come to the outskirt of the village to greet him with cowdung solution, broomstick and a garland of toru shoes, these the Holiyas say disarm the Brahmin of his evil *mana* and the Holiyas have little to fear consequent social intercourse with the Brahmins. The ignorance of the *mana* or *bonga* of a person makes a Ho of Chhota Nagpur avoid his contacts, and in hostels of aboriginal boys, there are innumerable food groups which maintain social distance as well as taboo commensality.

The principle of *mana* among the Hos of Chhota Nagpur, assumes the form of *Bongaism*. To the Hos, Banga as a power is unlimited in time and extensive in space. It has no particular shape or form. According to Majumdar, a *bonga* may inhabit a hill; the hill itself is not a Bonga. It may dwell in the river or in the rays of the sun, but the river or the rays by themselves cannot be described as *Bonga*. Further, a *Bonga* cannot be destroyed.

The concept of *mana* of *bonga* does explain the social distance and personality fixation. It has given birth to innumerable taboos and avoidances. It regulates individual behaviour and group responses, and its importance to tribal life and conduct must be conceded.

Thus, we find Bongaism in Chhota Nagpur is a *prima facie* factor in their tribal religion and exercises a strong influence over the life of the people.

In India, it was S.C. Roy to make an exhaustive survey of the *mana* principle from primitive to modern religions.

The principle of *mana* is recognized by almost all primitive tribes of the world. Among the Mongoloid tribes, notions analogous to the *mana* of Ocenia occur as also again among Indonesians and Melanesians. In Polynesia the concept of *mana* is both patent and latent and is recognized as a source of personal distinction, but there is no stratification as we find in India where it has made a major contribution in the development of caste feelings and keeping groups segregated from each other.

Theory of Naturism

As is usual with the theories that arise in reaction against some other, it was but natural that some theory may have come out as a result of reaction of animistic ideas. As the animistic theory of Tylor gives primacy to the worship of the soul, and derives the worship of nature from it, another school of thought associated with the name of German scholar, Max-Muller, reverses the orders and derives the belief in supernatural beings from the sensations aroused in man by overwhelming and at time catasysmic manifestations of nature. These, for being Natural, were calculated to make the mind aware of the "over-whelming pressure of the infinite".

In such experiences, in Max-Muller's opinion, who was the originator and propounder of the Naturalistic theory of religion, were the germs of religious experiences laid which grew into religion proper through a 'disease of language', so the scheme of Naturism would suggest.

Max-Muller holds that man first called the striking phenomena of nature by terms which denoted their activities – a "thunder bolt" was called that tears up the soil on that spreads fire, the wind, something that sighs and whistles" – (as quoted by Durkheim) – and so on.

This description of the phenomena of nature in terms of human or quasi-human activities led to an interpretation of them in anthropomorphic terms, and divine personalities were invented to account for the activities of natural phenomena.

The origin of religion, thus according to Naturism, lay in "disease of thought and of language", since the words used to describe the awe-inspiring phenomena of natural were terms denoting human activities, these terms were taken to imply the existence of personal agencies operative in the natural phenomena themselves. Thus we see that naturism attempted to discover the origin of religion in the phenomena of nature.

Conclusion

In conclusion, and summing up the various theories, we can say that it would be a mistake to regard any one of them as "the only" or the fundamental theory of religion and thus seeking for its universal application.

The effort for unilinearism in any direction would be unscientific. The more tangible solution seems in the realisation of the fact that various factors may at different times and place have been responsible for the birth and growth of a philosophy like that of religion – and there may have been rather a parallel development in the field of religion also than a unilinear order, as has been found in other fields of science.

With this attitude only we would be able to do justice to all the theories of religion discussed here.

Bibliography

Boas, Franz, *General Anthropology.*
Calverton (edited) : *Making of Man.*
Dube, S.C. : *Anthropology : The Study of Man.*
Ehrenfels : *Mother Right in India.*
Evanspiritchard, E.E. : *Social Anthropology.*
Goldenweiser, A.A. : *Anthropology.*
Hoebel, E.A. : *Man in the Primitive World.*
Hoebel, Jennings & Smith : *Reading in Anthropology.*
Kroeber, A.L. (edited) : *Anthropology-Today.*
Kroeber, A.L. : *Anthropology.*
Linton, Ralph (edited) : *Science of Man in the World Crisis.*
Lowie, R.H. : *Primitive Society.*
——— : *Primitive Religion.*
——— : *History of Ethnological Theory*
——— : *Social Organization.*
Majumdar and Madan Man, : *Introduction to Social Anthropology.*
Majumdar, D.N. : *Races and Cultures of India.*
Nadel, S.F. : *Foundations of Social Anthropology.*
Penniman, T.K. : *A Hundred Years of Anthropology.*
Piddington, Ralph : *An Introduction to Social Anthropology.*
Radcliffe, Brown, A.R. : *Structure and Function in Primitive Society.*

JOURNALS

Journal of Royal Anthropological Institute.

Index